The anti-tank regiments of the British Army entered the Second World War armed, for the most part, with the Ordnance Quick Firing (OQF) 2pdr, accepted by the War Office in 1935 and first allocated to operational units three years later (1). Although often criticised for its inability to penetrate the armour of the heavier German tanks, the gun's main drawbacks were its high silhouette and the lack of a high-explosive round. It was in fact superior in some ways to the 3.7cm Pak 36, the standard German anti-tank gun of the period.

In North Africa the 2pdr batteries were supplemented by 25pdr field guns, which were capable of operating in a direct fire role, until the arrival of the first 6pdr guns in early 1942. In the Western Desert it was found that the carriage of the 2pdr could be easily damaged as it was towed over the rough terrain and this gave rise to the practice of transporting the anti-tank guns *en portee*. The 2pdr guns were usually mounted on Ford 30cwt lorries and although the intention was that the trucks should only be used to transport the guns, firing from the vehicle became increasingly common (2). When the heavier 6pdr became available in 1942 it was carried by a 3-ton truck and while these arrangements had some initial success they were no match for a tank, despite their mobility. In addition, as they were largely unarmoured, they were vulnerable to machine-gun fire and at the beginning of 1943 it was decided to abandon the *en portee* concept, except in motorised infantry battalions.

But the notion of a self-propelled anti-tank gun had obviously taken root and at about this time the Deacon, a 6pdr gun mounted in a turret on the flatbed of an armoured AEC Matador truck, entered service in North Africa. These performed admirably at El Hamma in the battles for the Mareth Line in March 1943 but were not considered suitable for use in the coming campaign in northern Europe and were withdrawn from service (3). Meanwhile, the US Army, after studying the German Blitzkrieg tactics employed in the Polish and French campaigns, began the establishment of what became known as the Tank Destroyer Force. Reasoning that future b[...] involve large numbers of Ge[...] that would inevitably break [...] screen of towed anti-tank guns, the tank destroyers would need to be highly mobile, heavily armoured and capable of swift concentration. The mission of the tank destroyers was essentially defensive in nature, ideally firing into the flanks of an enemy armoured attack from defilade, and in this the US and British anti-tank doctrines were fundamentally similar.

The earliest equipment of the tank destroyer battalions were the 75mm M1987 mounted on an M3 half track, which was used with some success in Tunisia and the Pacific, and the 37mm anti-tank gun carried on the cargo platform of a Dodge ¾-ton truck. However, both these designs were viewed as expedients even at the time and the vehicle which would characterise the US Army tank destroyer units more than any other was the 3" Gun Motor Carriage M10, better known today, almost certainly incorrectly, as the Wolverine.

In Britain work had been going on for some time to find a suitable self-propelled platform for the powerful 17pdr gun and in October 1942 it was decided to progress with a design based on the chassis of a Valentine tank which would eventually become the Archer, entering service in late 1944. As something of a stopgap, the British Army began taking delivery of the American M10 in late 1943 eventually receiving a total of 1,650. Of these, all but 550 were converted to carry the OQF 17pdr, a high-velocity weapon which was capable of penetrating the armour of the heaviest German tanks. The resulting vehicle is today almost universally referred to as the Achilles and although this name was probably never employed during the war, I have used it throughout this book as it will be familiar to most readers. Interestingly, a number of British commanders, including Montgomery, felt that the development of new armoured vehicles was a waste of resources, considering the Sherman to be an all-round general purpose tank. But the high casualty rates suffered by the towed anti-tank gun batteries in the Normandy Bocage must surely attest to the worth of the self-propelled guns.

according to the weight of the projectile. The later 6pdr was built by the Americans, without its characteristic muzzle brake, as the 57mm anti-tank gun while the 17pdr of the Achilles was equivalent to 76.2mm. As a matter of convenience I have used the abbreviation pdr in place of pounder throughout this book.

2. The first use of British anti-tank guns carried on trucks may have occurred during the French campaign of 1940. However, the vehicles were probably not used as a firing platform.

3. The Deacons were manned by crews from ZZ Battery of 1st Royal Horse Artillery attached to 76th Anti-Tank Regiment for the final battles in North Africa. A few vehicles were converted to armoured ammunition carriers while others were sold to Turkey.

The first 17pdr guns to go into action were fitted to a 25pdr field gun carriage as an expedient and referred to by the codename Pheasant. This gun, with its barrel at full recoil, was photographed in Tunisia in 1943. Firing an armour-piercing projectile at a muzzle velocity of almost 3,000 feet per second the 17pdr gun was capable of penetrating the frontal armour of a German Panther tank at 1,000 metres.

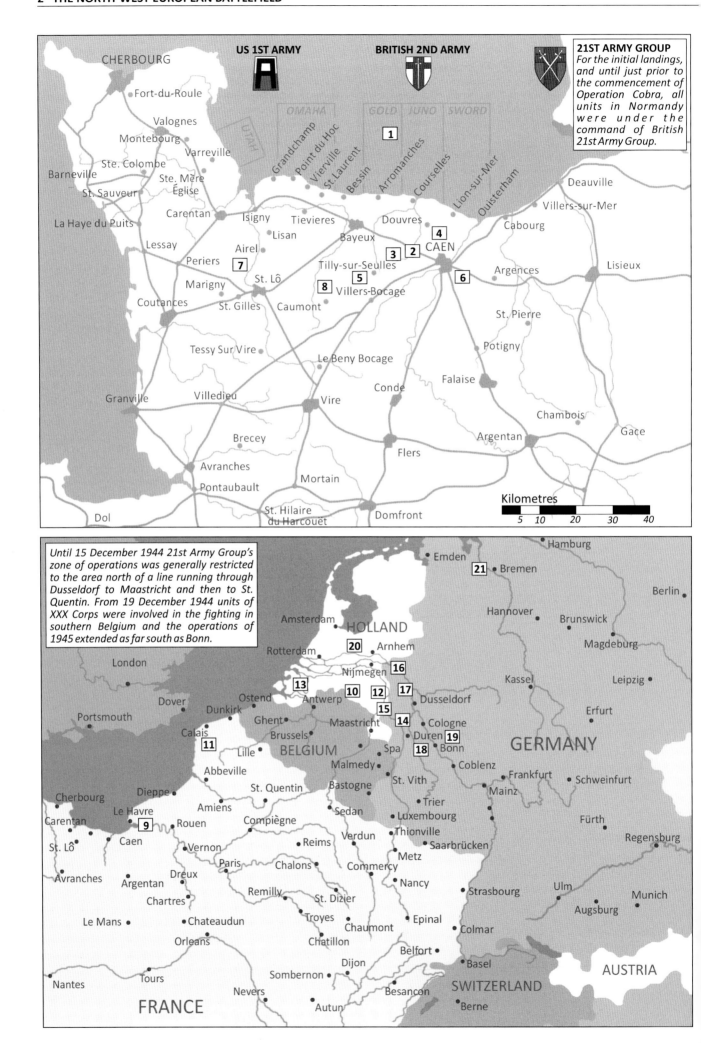

US 1ST ARMY

BRITISH 2ND ARMY

21ST ARMY GROUP
For the initial landings, and until just prior to the commencement of Operation Cobra, all units in Normandy were under the command of British 21st Army Group.

Until 15 December 1944 21st Army Group's zone of operations was generally restricted to the area north of a line running through Dusseldorf to Maastricht and then to St. Quentin. From 19 December 1944 units of XXX Corps were involved in the fighting in southern Belgium and the operations of 1945 extended as far south as Bonn.

The maps on the facing page indicate the general areas where major operations conducted by 21st Army Group took place. These actions, and other significant events, are discussed further in the timeline shown below and on the following pages. Note that the locations given, due to the limitations of space, are approximate only. Note also that the dates indicate when a particular operation began and some battles could last for several days or several weeks. At top: 1. Operation Overlord. 6 June 1944. 2. Operation Martlet (sometimes referred to as Operation Dauntless). 25 June 1944. 3. Operation Epsom. 26 June 1944. 4. Operation Charnwood. 8 July 1944. 5. Operation Pomegranate. 15 July 1944. 6. Operation Goodwood. 18 July 1944. 7. Operation Cobra. 25 July 1944. 8. Operation Bluecoat. 30 July 1944. At bottom: 9. Operation Astonia. 10 September 1944. 10. Operation Market-Garden. 17 September 1944. 11. Operation Undergo. 25 September 1944. 12. Operation Aintree. 30 September. 13. Operation Infatuate. 2 October 1944. 14. Operation Clipper. 18 November 1944. 15. Operation Blackcock. 14 January 1945. 16. Operation Veritable. 8 February 1945. 17. Operation Blockbuster. 3 March 1945. 18. Operation Plunder. 23 March 1945. 19. Operation Varsity. The airborne component of Operation Plunder. 20. Operation Anger. 11 April 1945. 21. Operation Bremen. 13 April 1945.

6 June 1944. Allied troops land on the Normandy beaches as part of Operation Overlord. Although the landings are immensely successful, the town of Caen, an important road junction on the Orne River just 12 kilometres from the coast, remains in German hands as night falls.

7 June 1944. The planned assault on Caen, codenamed Operation Perch, is held back by constant enemy counterattacks and hampered by the congestion on the beaches. Elsewhere, the Germans are able to deny Carpiquet airfield to the Canadians. Most of 7th Armoured Division is landed on this day and British XXX Corps captures Bayeux and Port-en-Bessin-Huppain.

8 June 1944. British and American units link up north of Bayeux.

9 June 1944. US troops capture St. Mère-Église. German aircraft attack the Orne River bridges but are driven off by anti-aircraft fire.

10 June 1944. To the west of Caen, 7th Armoured Division occupies Tilly-sur-Seulles late in the evening but it is retaken by the Germans on the next day.

11 June 1944. Units of British VIII Corps land in Normandy.

12 June 1944. Despite local German successes, British and US Army units are able to link up near Carentan creating a continuous front. Over 300,000 men and 50,000 vehicles have been landed since D-day.

13 June 1944. Elements of British 7th Armoured Division are severely mauled at Villers-Bocage by a single platoon of Tiger I tanks. On the same day, with no sign of the Germans giving way, Operation Perch is called off.

15 June 1944. The fighting for Tilly-sur-Suelles continues with the Germans gradually reinforcing their positions around the town. tanks of Panzer-Regiment 6 added to the defence.

25 June 1944. Before dawn, Operation Martlet, a limited assault made by units of British XXX Corps to capture Rauray and the German positions around Noyers west of Caen, is launched. The offensive was meant to secure the flank of Operation Epsom.

26 June 1944. The British commence Operation Epsom, an attempt to outflank the German defenders of Caen and secure the city. After two days of costly fighting Caen remains in German hands.

27 June 1944. The tanks of the British 11th Armoured Division overrun much of Hill 112, the highest point on the Normandy battlefield, south-west of Caen. During the afternoon the Germans make a determined counterattack and the summit is re-occupied as night falls. On the same day Operation Mitten, a limited assault to reduce a German salient based around the Chateaux of la Londe and la Landel north of Caen, is launched. The official British history dubbed this area 'the bloodiest square mile in Normandy'.

29 June 1944. Suspecting that a strong counterattack is imminent, all British armoured units around Hill 112 withdraw, allowing the Germans to occupy the area without loss.

30 June 1944. Although the expected German counterattacks are beaten off, Operation Epsom is effectively ended. Ultimately unsuccessful, Martlet and Epsom had nevertheless inflicted heavy casualties on the German defenders, particularly the armoured units, which are relegated to static defence. This engagement is sometimes referred to as the First Battle of the Odon.

1 July 1944. Unknown to the Allies the Germans decide to gradually evacuate and eventually abandon Caen, transferring their remaining armoured units to the west to meet the expected threat from the Americans.

8 July 1944. British 2nd Army launches Operation Charnwood, a combined assault to take Caen.

9 July 1944. British and Canadian units fight their way into Caen and manage to secure the northern suburbs although the Germans stubbornly cling to the southern half.

10 July 1944. A major British assault captures Hill 112 after heavy fighting. The next day, a German counterattack drives the British from the summit of Hill 112. To the west, US troops enter St. Lô.

15 July 1944. Units of British XII Corps advance towards Hill 112 as part of an operation codenamed Greenline, designed to draw the German's attention away from preparations for the upcoming Operation Goodwood. Just before midnight, British XXX Corps commences Operation Pomegranate aimed at the high ground north-east of Villers Bocage.

16 July 1944. A German counterattack to the west of Villers-Bocage is beaten back with heavy loss.

18 July 1944. Operation Goodwood begins, preceded by a massive aerial bombardment. British VIII Corps, with the bulk of the armour, was to advance from the Orne bridgehead and capture Bretteville-sur-Laize, Vimont and Argences and head directly south towards Falaise destroying as many German armoured vehicles in the process as possible. However, in the fighting around Bouguébus the British and Canadians lose 100 tanks.

19 July 1944. Canadian units clear the southern suburbs of Caen. British tanks enter Bras and Hubert-Folie on the outskirts of the town.

20 July 1944. Operation Goodwood ends, in large part due to the weather, with the British armoured units in possession of Bourguébus Ridge. This was the largest tank battle fought by the British Army during the Second World War. On the same day the Germans launch a major attack west of Bouguébus, parallel to the Caen-Falaise road. At Rastenburg in East Prussia, an attempt is made on Hitler's life.

25 July 1944. The US Army's Operation Cobra begins. After a slow start the Americans advance rapidly towards their objectives. On the same day the Canadians attack German positions south of Caen as part of Operation Spring.

28 July 1944. American units capture Coutances, about 40 kilometres west of St-Lô, but are held up outside the town.

30 July 1944. To support Operation Cobra, British 2nd Army launches a large-scale attack codenamed Bluecoat. On the same day as the offensive begins American forces capture Avranches. British troops attack Caumont, situated between St. Lô and Villiers-Bocage.

4 August 1944. Hill 112 is occupied by British units after the German defenders abandon their positions. In the fighting here Bombadier Stanley 'Jock' Campbell of Z Battery, 21st Anti-Tank Regiment destroys three German tanks and disables a fourth with just four shots and repels a force of enemy infantrymen with small arms fire. For his actions on this day Bombadier Campbell is later awarded the Military Medal. On the following day British units secure Mount Pinçon, beating of a strong German counterattack. This action effectively brings Operation Bluecoat to an end.

6 August 1944. Just before midnight, the Germans launch Operation Lüttich, an ambitious attack intended to blunt the US Army's Cobra offensive and retake Avranches. Aided by the weather, the Panzers make some early tactical gains, including the capture of Mortain.

8 August 1944. With the Germans stalled at Mortain, the British launch Operation Totalise with fresh Canadian and Polish units attacking towards Falaise. That afternoon, the Americans occupy Le Mans.

9 August 1944. The Germans counterattack north-east of Falaise, claiming the destruction of twenty-eight Canadian tanks without loss.

10 August 1944. Canadian units reach Hill 195, just north of Falaise.

11 August 1944. In an attempt to cut off the German units withdrawing from the Mortain area, the British mount an attack towards Moncy on the Vire to Saint-Germain-du-Crioult road. Meeting fierce resistance, the attack bogs down after advancing just 800 metres.

14 August 1944. British troops launch Operation Tractable towards Falaise, preceded by an intense aerial bombardment.

15 August 1944. As part of Operation Dragoon, Allied units begin landing in the south of France.

17 August 1944. Canadian troops enter Falaise threatening the German Army in Normandy with encirclement.

19 August 1944. Polish armoured units link up with US troops at Chambois just south of Mont Ormel as evening approaches.

20 August 1944. During the early morning, the Germans mount an attack towards the Polish positions on Mont Ormel. By noon a fresh German assault manages to break through the Polish front as Canadian reinforcements are held up further to the north. Within a few hours approximately 10,000 Germans are able to escape from the Falaise Pocket.

21 August 1944. During the early evening Polish and Canadian troops meet at Coudehard, north-east of Trun, closing the German escape route for the last time.

25 August 1944. Allied units enter Paris, the final objective of Operation Overlord.

10 September 1944. Operation Astonia, the assault on the French port city of Le Havre commences.

17 September 1944. Operation Market-Garden, a combined Allied land and airborne attempt to cross the lower Rhine at Arnhem in the Netherlands, begins. After a promising start the advance is soon stalled.

25 September 1944. Operation Market-Garden is officially brought to an end. On the same day Operation Undergo, the assault on Calais, begins.

30 September 1944. Operation Aintree, the battle to secure the towns of Overloon and Venray in the Netherlands, commences. Resisting stubbornly, the Germans manage to hold their positions here until mid-October.

2 October 1944. Operation Infatuate, the final assault on the German defences in the Scheldt Estuary, begins. The last Germans, principally naval artillerymen, did not surrender until the second week of November.

21 October 1944. Aachen is captured, earning the distinction of being the first German city to fall to the Western Allies.

31 October 1944. British units reach the river Maas, south of Rotterdam and establish a bridgehead.

An M10 tank destroyer of 67 Battery, 20th Anti-Tank Regiment photographed on Sword Beach during the early morning hours of 6 June 1944. The anti-tank units of the three assault divisions were all supplied with a self-propelled element as it was feared that the towed guns would too easily become bogged and obstruct the following waves. This vehicle is also shown and discussed in the Camouflage & Markings section on page 17 and may be the M10 seen in the background in the photograph on page 9.

Photographed near the town of Goch in western Germany, this Achilles 17pdr is from Y Battery, 21st Anti-Tank Regiment. Note the so-called duckbill extenders on the tracks and part of the deep wading gear covering the exhaust on the lower hull. The Guards formation badge is visible on the left-hand side of the hull rear plate and the Arm of Service sign with a white number 77 identifying an anti-tank regiment of an armoured division can be seen on the right. Next to the latter, just visible, is an RA tactical sign denoting the first gun of F Troop.

1 November 1944. British units land on Walcheren in the Scheldt Estuary.

2 November 1944. US Army units move to attack the Roer Dams along the German-Belgian frontier.

4 November 1944. An ad-hoc German armoured force begins a series of counterattacks against US units in the Roer Dams region.

9 November 1944. The last German units on Walcheren surrender. The Moerdijk bridgehead across the Meuse river is evacuated.

11 November 1944. Advancing rapidly, US units capture three bridgeheads over the Moselle.

17 November 1944. Elements of the US 3rd Army cross the German frontier cutting off the fortress city of Metz.

18 November 1944. Operation Clipper, an assault to reduce the Geilenkirchen salient on the Dutch-German frontier east of Jülich, commences.

19 November 1944. US units fight their way into the suburbs of Metz. The French 1st Armoured Division reaches the Rhine. German units counterattack near Merzenhausen and around Tripsrath north of Geilenkircken.

24 November 1944. The allies cross the River Saar near the German border.

8 December 1944. German troops evacuate Jülich on the Roer river.

10 December 1944. Hagenau and Saargemünd, between Saarbrücken and Strasbourg, are captured by the Allies.

13 December 1944. German 7.Armee withdraws into the fortified positions of the Westwall.

16 December 1944. The Germans launch Wacht am Rhein, their last major operation in the West. Achieving complete surprise, the German offensive manages to break through the American lines on a 70-mile front. However, difficult terrain and poor weather hamper the German units and ominously none reach their assigned first-day objectives.

18 December 1944. After less than 48 hours all German units are reporting shortages of fuel.

19 December 1944. US units come under attack at Dom Bütgenbach, less than 10 kilometres east of Malmedy. On the following morning the Germans capture Stavelot.

21 December 1944. Although US Army units retake Stavelot, Bastogne is besieged and German units capture St. Vith while the attacks on Dom Bütgenbach continue. On the same day elements of British XXX Corps are ordered to move south and block the German units heading towards the Meuse.

22 December 1944. The reconnaissance battalion of 2.Panzer-Division breaches the American line and advances towards Buissonville and the Meuse crossing.

24 December 1944. British tanks cross the Meuse and run head-on into the advancing Germans. Supported by US armoured units and the fighter-bombers of the RAF they halt the German column and secure Buissonville. On the following day the lead German elements are surrounded and destroyed despite a determined relief effort.

30 December 1944. German units launch a heavy attack on the Bastogne corridor. The British attack on Houffalize, north-east of Bastogne, is halted by determined German resistance.

31 December 1944. Further to the south German units launch Operation Nordwind, an attack towards Strasbourg in the Saar valley.

3 January 1945. British counterattacks begin on the northern side of the Ardennes salient.

5 January 1945. Although Operation Nordwind quickly becomes bogged down, a supplementary assault manages to create a bridgehead on the Rhine between Strasbourg and Hagenau.

8 January 1945. Hitler orders the withdrawal of all German units from the Ardennes salient.

9 January 1945. In what is virtually the last gasp of Operation Nordwind, an ad-hoc German force launches an attack against Hatten, south of Oldenburg.

12 January 1945. Operation Nordwind is decisively halted less than 10 kilometres from Strasbourg. British and US Army forces link up near La-Roche-en-Ardenne, north west of Houffulize.

14 January 1945. Operation Blackcock, a major assault undertaken by units of British 2nd Army to clear the so-called Roer Triangle west of Erkelenz, begins.

4 February 1945. The last German troops leave Belgium.

8 February 1945. British and Canadian troops launch Operation Veritable, a month-long battle through the Reichswald ending at Xanten on the west bank of the Rhine. The attack was co-ordinated with the US Army's Operation Grenade.

9 February 1945. The last Rhine bridge is destroyed in the Colmar Pocket after much of 19.Armee has been evacuated.

10 February 1945. US units capture the last of the Ruhr dams.

12 February 1945. British and Canadian troops capture Cleve.

17 February 1945. US 3rd Army breaks through the Siegfried Line and advances into Germany.

23 February 1945. US 9th Army attacks from the Roer bridgehead towards the Hürtgen Forest but is bogged down in savage fighting.

28 February 1945. US units in the Hürtgen Forest break through near Erkelenz, west of Cologne, at great cost.

3 March 1945. Units of 1st Canadian Army and British XXX Corps begin Operation Blockbuster, the last phase of Operation Veritable.

6 March 1945. Cologne surrenders. During the next day the Rhine bridge at Remagen is captured intact.

9 March 1945. The US Third Army captures Andernach on the Rhine.

14 March 1945. US Army units cross the Moselle.

15 March 1945. Attempts by the Americans to expand the Remagen bridgehead fail.

17 March 1945. The Remagen bridge collapses.

20 March 1945. Saarbrücken falls to the Allies.

22 March 1945. Units of the US 3rd Army cross the Rhine at Oppenheim south of Mainz against ineffective German resistance.

23 March 1945. British and Canadian units begin their assault across the Rhine between Emmerich and Wesel, north of Essen, as part of Operation Plunder. The airborne component of this attack was referred to as Operation Varsity.

25 March 1945. British troops capture Wesel after an aerial bombardment almost completely destroys the town. On the following day Main and Darmstadt fall to US troops

27 March 1945. After fierce fighting US Army units capture Aschaffenburg.

28 March 1945. British troops begin their drive towards the Elbe as the US Army captures Marburg and Limburg.

1 April 1945. Two US armies link up at Lippstadt cutting off over 300,000 German troops in the Ruhr area.

2 April 1945. The British 7th Armoured Division reaches the Dortmund-Ems canal and over the next week the Allies capture Recklinghausen, Fulda and Kassel and Karlsruhe on the upper Rhine

11 April 1945. Operation Anger, an assault across the Nederrijn to capture Arnhem, commences. On the same day British units take Celle, near Hannover, cutting the road to Hamburg and US Army units reach Schweinfurt.

13 April 1945. Operation Bremen, the assault to capture the city, begins. The US 3rd Army captures Erfurt. On the following day US units capture Gera and Bayreuth.

15 April 1945. Arnhem is finally secured by the Canadians.

16 April 1945. US 1st Army captures Solingen and Wuppertal.

17 April 1945. British units attempt to outflank Soltau but are repulsed by a lone Tiger tank.

18 April 1945. An ad-hoc German armoured formation manages to drive the British from their positions around Wittingen. The US Army takes Magdeburg, Düsseldorf and Nürnberg. American units advance into western Czechoslovakia. The British capture Ülzen and Lüneburg.

19 April 1945. British troops launch an attack on Bremen. Leipzig and Halle fall to the Americans

21 April 1945. German tanks cut the Gifhorn-Brome road south of Wittingen, surprising US units who mistake them for Americans. French units capture Stuttgart although the Germans continue to resist around Elbingerode in the Harz Mountains.

22 April 1945. US 7th Army captures a bridge across the Danube. British troops reach Bremen. The next day, Dessau and Harburg are cleared of German troops and Frankfurt is captured.

24 April 1945. British and Canadian troops enter Bremen but the defenders hold out for a further 48 hours. US units cross the Danube at Dillingen and capture Ulm.

25 April 1945. US and Soviet units meet on the Elbe at Torgau south-west of Berlin.

26 April 1945. US troops take Regensburg on the Danube.

28 April 1945. The Canadians capture Emden and Wilhelmshaven, while US units take Augsburg and reach the Austrian border.

29 April 1945. Under heavy fire, including an attack by Stuka dive-bombers, British troops cross the Elbe near Hamburg.

30 April 1945. Hitler commits suicide, appointing Grossadmiral Karl Dönitz as his successor. US and Soviet units meet at Ellenburg, south of Berlin.

1 May 1945. The single Tiger tank which had stopped the British armoured advance near Wittingen, again manages to halt a complete tank regiment outside Schwarzenbek, east of Hamburg.

2 May 1945. Elements of British VIII Corps reach Lübeck on the Baltic coast.

3 May 1945. Hamburg is declared an open city and surrenders to the British. US troops reach the Brenner Pass on the Italian border.

4 May 1945. Admiral Hans-Georg von Friedeburg, representing the German government, arrives at Field Marshal Montgomery's headquarters to surrender all German forces in Holland, North-west Germany and Denmark. Elsewhere, the US 7th Army takes Innsbruck, Salzburg and Berchtesgarten.

5 May 1945. The US 3rd Army takes Pilsen in Czechoslovakia and prepares to drive towards Prague.

7 May 1945. Generaloberst Jodl, as OKW Chief of Staff, signs Germany's unconditional surrender. All operations are to cease at one minute after midnight the next day.

In 1939, when the war began, the Royal Artillery controlled 100 anti-tank batteries that were either with active formations or were in the process of being formed. These were, for the most part, equipped with the 2pdr anti-tank gun which had entered service in 1935. This gun soon proved to be at a severe disadvantage when pitted against the German Panzers and its replacement by the 6pdr had in fact been on the drawing board since 1938. The Ordnance Quick-Firing (OQF) 6pdr was a British version of the US Army's 57mm gun and although it was a marked improvement on the 2pdr, it would not reach front-line units until April 1942, by which time the Germans were able to field more heavily armoured tanks.

Unlike the artillery's field batteries the anti-tank units went through several organisational changes after the French campaign of 1940, some reflecting advances in weapons technology and the introduction of efficient self-propelled mounts, but mainly due to the diversity of equipment within the individual regiments.

Experience gained in North Africa also played a part and by September 1943, a four-battery regiment was standard. An anti-tank battery contained three troops and regiments attached to armoured divisions were each made up of two batteries equipped with twelve 6pdr guns and two batteries each comprising twelve M10 tank destroyers. Those units attached to the various corps were organised in the same manner. The anti-tank regiments of infantry divisions contained four batteries each with eight 6pdr guns and four of the new OQF 17pdr models which had first seen action in Tunisia, mounted on a 25pdr field gun carriage. The 17pdr was capable of penetrating the thickest German armour but, as is often the case with direct-fire weapons, its operation left the crews dreadfully exposed and they suffered disproportionately high casualties in Normandy.

Further changes introduced in January 1944 permitted divisional anti-tank regiments to be organised with either four batteries of eight 6pdr and four 17pdr guns or four batteries of eight 6pdr guns and four M10 tank destroyers or two batteries with twelve 6pdr guns and two batteries each with twelve M10s. For whatever reason these establishments were almost immediately deemed to be unsuitable and as more 17pdr guns and self-propelled vehicles became available, new orders were issued. Regiments attached to armoured divisions would now contain two batteries equipped with the 17pdr and two batteries of M10s while the regiments of infantry divisions were made up of four batteries, each with eight 17pdr and four 6pdr guns. As before, the regiments attached to a corps were organised identically to the units allocated to armoured divisions.

In February or March 1944 a specialised organisation was approved for the D-Day assault infantry divisions where each battery contained one troop of M10 tank destroyers and two troops equipped with towed 6pdr guns. It was also at about this time that the regiments attached to armoured formations and corps headquarters began to receive the Achilles. The assault infantry organisation proved so successful that in August 1944 anti-tank regiments of infantry divisions began to be reorganised with one troop of 6pdr, one troop of 17pdr and one troop of

In the foreground, infantrymen, probably from the 2nd Battalion of the East Yorkshire Regiment, take shelter behind a carrier marked with the formation badge of 3rd Infantry Division. This regiment came ashore at Sword Beach in the second assault wave on 6 June 1944 and the photograph was taken at about 9.00am. The M10 from 20th Anti-Tank Regiment in the background is fitted with a deep wading stack and other photographs suggest that this may be the vehicle depicted at the bottom of page 17 in the Camouflage & Markings section.

An M10 tank destroyer of 20th Anti-Tank Regiment with men from 3rd Infantry Division photographed a short distance inland from Sword Beach on 6 June 1944. Note the brackets on the transmission cover that hold the spare wheels in place and the large white recognition star, partly obscured by ammunition and fuel containers. Part of the deep wading stack can be seen on the hull rear.

Notes

1. The Archer was based on the Valentine chassis and is in fact referred to as 'Valentine SP' throughout the regiment's war diary.

2. Sanna's Post referred to an engagement in which the battery took part during the Second Boer War. The honour title of Minden was conferred on 2 Battery in 1926 and celebrates the battle of Minden fought on 1 August 1759. The title is retained to this day by 12 (Minden) Anti-Tank Battery. Hulbert, an officer of the Territorial Army, had risen from the rank of temporary Captain to command the regiment and remained in the regular army after the war.

3. Confusingly, self-propelled guns are usually referred to in unit diaries as simply 'SP' or 'M10' without any mention of their armament.

self-propelled 17pdr guns. From October 1944 the latter were increasingly the Valentine 17pdr, usually referred to today as the Archer. Listed below are brief descriptions of the anti-tank regiments of the Royal artillery that served in northern Europe during the last year of the war. Note that only those units where the M10 or Achilles is specifically mentioned were equipped with those vehicles.

20th Anti-Tank Regiment, RA. Formed in 1938 from elements of 20th Field Brigade the regiment was made up of Batteries 41, 45, 67 and 101 and was attached to 3rd Infantry Division from 1939 until the end of the war. As part of one of the designated D-Day assault divisions the regiment was reorganised in early to give each battery a troop of M10 tank destroyers. This establishment is shown in some detail in the chart on the following page.

The regiment took part in the fighting in Normandy and the advance through France and later in Belgium and Holland. In late 1944 it was decided that the regiment's M10 tank destroyers would be replaced by the new Archer self-propelled 17pdr guns which were just coming into service and despite the objections of the commanding officer, who suggested that the M10s be retained as a divisional reserve, the conversion began in January 1945.

The first of the new vehicles went to 67 Battery and it was intended that 101 Battery would eventually be equipped entirely with the Archer while the remaining three batteries would each have

one troop of self-propelled guns and two troops of towed 17pdr guns. The regiment's Crusaders were to be replaced with Valentine XI OP tanks (1).

In the event this reorganisation took some time to accomplish and although it had probably been largely completed by April 1945 there is some evidence that a number of M10s were still on hand at that time. The regiment took part in the Rhine crossing operations and the battles in Germany and was near Bremen when the war ended.

21st Anti-Tank Regiment, RA. Raised from parts of 21st Field Brigade in 1938 the regiment was initially attached to 1st Infantry Division before joining the newly-formed Guards Armoured Division in 1941. By 1944 the regiment, commanded by Lieutenant Colonel R. C. Hulbert, was made up of Q (Sanna's Post) Battery, Y Battery, Z Battery and 2 (Minden) Battery (2).

For the campaign in France the regiment was equipped with a number of M10 tank destroyers and these were concentrated in Q and Y Batteries. The exact composition of the batteries is not known but 21st Army Group records state the each of the three armoured divisions was equipped with twelve M10 3", twelve M10 17pdr and twenty-four towed 17pdr guns (3). It seems that the Guards, unlike the other divisions, mixed their self-propelled guns and it is possible that the SP batteries contained two of each type. The names given to the regiment's M10 3" vehicles would seem to confirm this with known examples

............text continued on page 10

ANTI-TANK REGIMENT, ASSAULT INFANTRY DIVISION. JUNE 1944

For the Normandy landings 3rd Infantry Division, 50th (Northumbrian) Division and 3rd Canadian Division were designated Assault Divisions and the anti-tank regiments of each were allocated one troop of M10 tank destroyers per battery. The exact organisations varied and that shown here depicts 20th Anti-Tank Regiment of 3rd Infantry Division which landed on Sword Beach. For the actual landing 245 Battery of 62 Anti-Tank Regiment, equipped with twelve 17pdr self-propelled guns, was attached to the regiment.

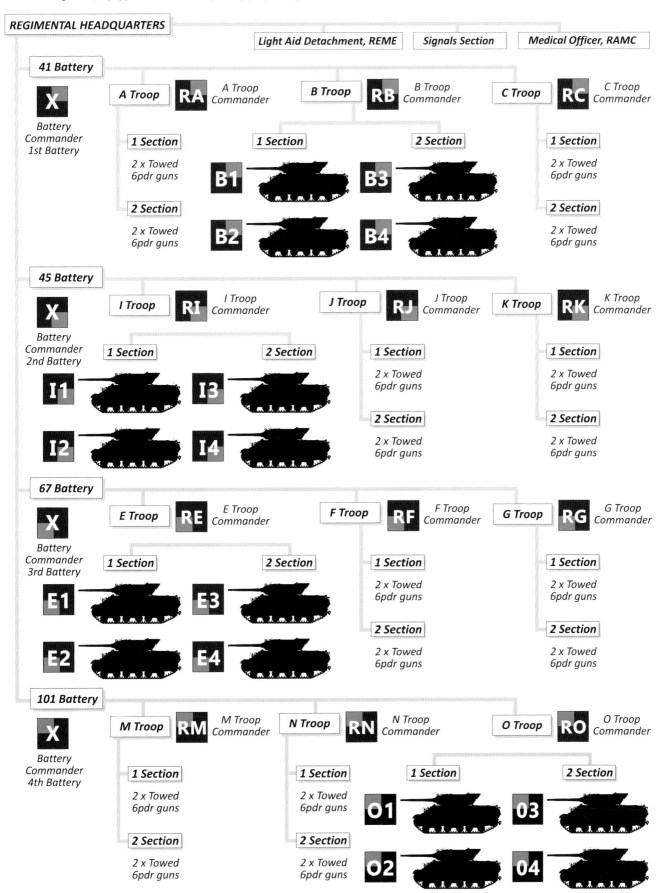

Full-colour versions of the tactical signs used by the Royal Artillery are shown in the Camouflage & Markings section of this book which begins on page 17.

...........text continued from page 8

Notes

1. All regiments raised from Territorial Army formations were distinguisghed by the suffix TA as used here.

being Ajax, Avalanche, Bahram, Bulldog and Corsair, all from Q Battery. The regiment arrived in Normandy on 23 June 1944 and in the following days went into action for the first time, coming up against a number of German tanks near Cheux, between Tilly-sur-Seulles and Bretteville-sur-Odon, and later taking part in the fighting for the Caen canal at Benouville in early July.

After the battles in Normandy the regiment was engaged in the advance into Belgium and in the fighting in Holland as part of Operation Market-Garden. With the tanks of 5th Guards Armoured Brigade the regiment fought in the Ardennes during the bitterly cold winter months when the engines of the self-propelled mountings had to be started every hour to prevent them from freezing.

In early 1945, 21st Anti-Tank Regiment took part in Operation Veritable, the battle to clear the Reichswald, and the advance into Germany. When the war ended the regiment was near Cuxhaven, north-west of Hamburg at the mouth of the Elbe River.

52nd (6th London) Anti-Tank Regiment, RA (TA).
Formed in 1938 from parts of the London Regiment, a unit of the Territorial Army, which was disbanded in the same year (1). The regiment contained Batteries 205, 206, 207 and 208 and served as part of the BEF, in India, Iraq, Sicily and Italy until March 1945 when it was transferred to northern Europe as part of 5th Infantry Division. The regiment was completely equipped with towed guns.

54th (Queen's Own Glasgow Yeomanry) Anti-Tank Regiment, RA (TA).
Attached to the 52nd (Lowland) Infantry Division this regiment contained Batteries 214 (Queen's Own Royal Glasgow Yeomanry), 215 (5th City of Glasgow), 295 and 304. On 14 December 1944 the regiment received notice that it would be reorganised with its four batteries each made up of one troop of 6pdr guns towed by carriers, one troop of towed 17pdr guns and one troop of Archer 17pdr self-propelled guns.

A report of April 1945 mentions that one M22 Locust airborne light tank, presumably used as a command vehicle, was on hand.

55th (Suffolk and Norfolk Yeomanry) Anti-Tank Regiment, RA (TA).
Formed from the Suffolk and Norfolk Yeomanry and attached to 49th Infantry Division, the regiment was made up from Batteries 217 and 218 (Suffolk), 219 and 220 (Norfolk).

In line with the reorganisation introduced for the anti-tank regiments of infantry divisions, one troop in each battery was to be equipped with Archer 17pdr self-propelled guns. The first vehicles arrived on 4 November and were allocated to 219 Battery and by the end of the year the other batteries had received the allocation of Archers.

In February 1945, 219 and 218 Batteries gave up the last of their 6pdrs and were organised with two troops of towed 17pdrs and one troop of self-propelled 17pdr guns.

M10 tank destroyers of 21st Anti-Tank Regiment, RA photographed in the Norman countryside on 20 July 1944. The formation badge of the Guards Armoured Division is just visible on the rear of the hull on the left hand side. Note the exhaust shroud and metal frame for the deep wading stack at the hull rear. This arrangement is also shown in the Camouflage & Markings section. Note also the field-modified extension on the hull rear holding the crew's belongings. This vehicle is fitted with the T51 rubber block tracks.

Photographed during the advance south of Caumont-l'Éventé in Normandy on 31 July 1944, this Achilles 17pdr self-propelled gun is almost certainly from one of the batteries of 21st Anti-Tank Regiment. Note that a number of the track grousers, normally held in the rack on the hull side, have been replaced by jerry cans.

Taken from the same sequence as the image shown above, this photograph provides a good view of one of several types of arrangements for hold the deep wading stack in place. Here also the track grousers serve merely as a means of securing fuel containers. The white tape indicates that this area has been cleared of mines.

............text continued from page 8

Notes

1. All regiments raised from Territorial army formations were distinguished by the suffix TA as used here.

59th (Duke of Connaught's Hampshire) Anti-Tank Regiment, RA (TA). Formed from 6th (Duke of Connaught's Own) Battalion, The Hampshire Regiment in 1938 and attached to 43rd (Wessex) Infantry Division, this regiment contained Batteries 233, 235, 236 and 333.

From early December 1944 the regiment was equipped with Archer 17pdr self-propelled guns, the first vehicles going to 333 Battery, and Valentine OP tanks.

61st Anti-Tank Regiment, RA (TA). Formed by renaming 51st Anti-Tank Regiment in 1939 and comprising Batteries 241, 242, 243 and 244, this regiment was initially subordinated to 9th Infantry Division until 1940 when it was attached to 51st (Highland) Infantry Division.

The regiment took part in the fighting in Normandy and the capture of Le Havre and the Battle of the Scheldt. During October 1944, 245 Battery of 62nd Anti-Tank Regiment, with its Achilles 17pdr tank destroyers, was attached to the regiment. By February 1945 each of the

regiment's batteries had received a troop of Archer 17pdr self-propelled guns and it seems that by this time the regiment's towed 6pdr guns had all been replaced by the 17pdr.

The division's final situation report dated June 1945 shows five 'Valentine 6pdr' and three 'Valentine 75mm' on hand with 61st Anti-Tank Regiment and these were probably used as command tanks.

62nd Anti-Tank Regiment, RA (TA). Formed in 1939 by renaming 52nd Anti-Tank Regiment, this unit contained Batteries 245, 246, 247 and 248 and was originally attached to 4th (London) Infantry Division. By 1943 the regiment was subordinated directly to I Corps headquarters and was temporarily attached to 3rd Canadian Division for the D-Day landings.

By the time of the Normandy invasion, 245 Battery was equipped with Achilles 17pdr self-propelled guns, 246 and 247 Batteries had towed 17pdr guns towed by Crusader gun tractors and 248 Battery was outfitted with M10 tank destroyers.

............text continued on page 14

An M10 tank destroyer and, just visible, a Sherman tank said to have been photographed on the Vassy road during Operation Bluecoat on 4 August 1944. The vehicles in the background carry the formation badge of the Guards Armoured Division, which was responsible for this section of the assault, and it is likely that this M10 is from 21st Anti-tank Regiment. The use of the US Army tank helmet by M10 and Achilles British crews, as seen on the driver here, was not uncommon in North-Western Europe.

ANTI-TANK REGIMENT, CORPS HEADQUARTERS TROOPS. JULY 1944

Each of the four corps headquarters of British 2nd Army was allocated an anti-tank regiment and these formations, together with the regiments attached to the armoured divisions, began to replace their M10 tank destroyers with the 17pdr-armed version, better known today as the Achilles, shortly before D-Day. Although the organisation of some regiments differed slightly the unit shown here, 62nd Anti-Tank Regiment, was typical with two self-propelled batteries and two batteries of towed 17pdr guns. The first battery of this regiment came ashore on 6 June 1944 in support of 3rd Infantry Division.

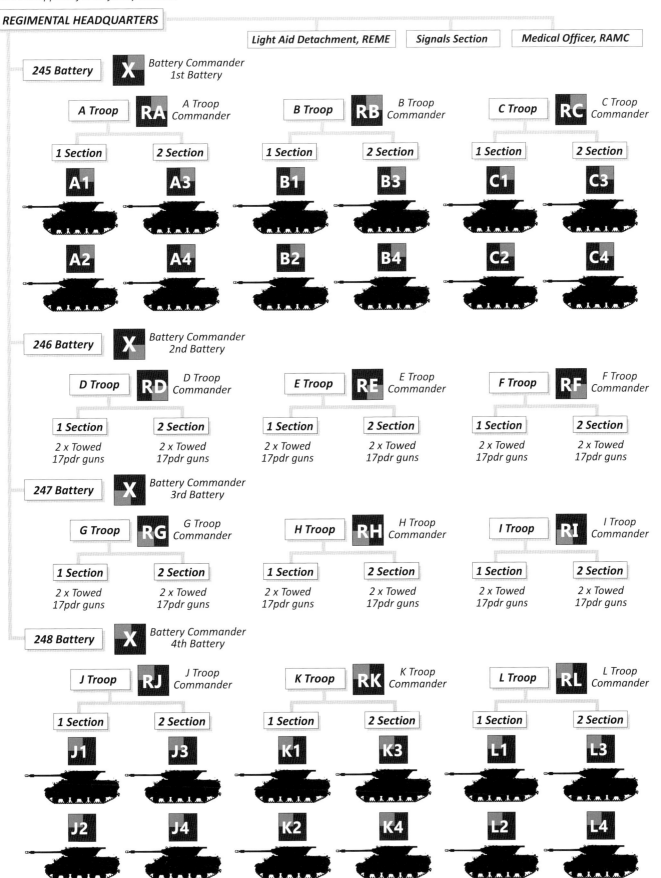

Full-colour versions of the tactical signs used by the Royal Artillery are shown in the Camouflage & Markings section of this book which begins on page 17.

Churchill tanks of 6th Guards Tank Brigade, with US paratroopers on board, pass an Achilles from what is almost certainly 63rd Anti-Tank Regiment near Dorsten in Germany on 28 March 1945. At this time the regiment, together with the Guards, 6th Field Regiment, 77th Medium Regiment, 3rd Reconaissance Regiment and the US 513th Parachute Regiment, formed the 6th Guards Armoured Brigade Group.

............text continued from page 12

Notes

1. Some sources suggest that 146 Battery was fully equipped with the Achilles in June 1944 while the regiment contained another three troops of M10 tank destroyers, presumably with 144 Battery. The regimental diary is of little help referring to all self-propelled guns as simply 'M.10'. There is, however, a mention of a G Troop vehicle that was lost to a mine in late October from which the firing mechanism of a 17pdr was retrieved. This would seem to confirm that the Achilles were concentrated in 146 Battery.

The 'Crusader command tanks' mentioned in the regimental diary were probably Crusader anti-aircraft tanks which were increasingly used as OP vehicles at this time. The organisation of this regiment is shown in detail in the chart on page 13.

63rd (Oxfordshire Yeomanry) Anti-Tank Regiment, RA (TA). Formed in 1939 from 211 and 212 Batteries, both raised from the Queen's Own Oxfordshire Hussars Yeomanry, the regiment was reorganised with 249, 250, 251 and 252 Batteries and was initially attached to 61st infantry Division.

In September 1944 the regiment was sent to France and was originally under the direct command of British 2nd Army headquarters but was later subordinated to VIII and I Corps.

In December 1944, 250 and 252 Batteries were disbanded and replaced by 144 and 146 Batteries of 91st (Argyll and Sutherland Highlanders) Anti-Tank Regiment which were equipped with M10 tank destroyers and Achilles 17pdr self-propelled guns (1).

As the new batteries had both been raised from battalions of the Argyll and Sutherland Highlanders, there was some concern over how the regiment should be referred to and it was decided that 249 and 251 Batteries should incorporate Oxfordshire Yeomanry into their titles while the new units would be known as 144 and 146 (Argyll and Sutherland

Highlanders) Batteries. All personnel continued to wear the dress distinctions and cap badges they had worn prior to the reorganisation. The regiment would henceforth be simply called 63rd Anti-Tank Regiment, RA.

65th (Suffolk and Norfolk) Anti-Tank Regiment, RA (TA). Formed in 1939 from elements of 55th Anti-Tank Regiment this unit served with 50th Infantry Division and for a time with 4th Indian Division.

From 1942 the regiment was attached to 7th Armoured Division and fought in North Africa, Sicily and Italy before returning to Britain in early 1944.

For the Normandy campaign the regiment's 257 and 259 Batteries were equipped with towed 17pdr guns while 258 and 260 Batteries were outfitted with M10 tank destroyers. Just six weeks before the D-Day landings 260 Battery was re-equipped with the Achilles 17pdr self-propelled gun.

The regiment took part in the Normandy battles, including the fighting around Villers-Bocage, Operation Goodwood, Operation Bluecoat and the subsequent pursuit to the Seine.

In late 1944 the regiment was engaged in Holland and in the spring of 1945 took part in the Rhine crossing operations and the battles in the Teutoberger Wald, pushing into Germany and ending the war near Kiel.

............text continued on page 50

The crew of this M10 tank destroyer are shown checking the bearings of the rear idler axle in August 1944. The cap badges identify this unit as 65th (Norfolk Yeomanry) Anti-Tank Regiment of 7th Armoured Division. Of note are the non-standard hooks on the turret and hull sides and also the small fillets on the suspension's return roller arms.

Heavily-camouflaged Achilles 17pdr self-propelled guns photographed in the streets of Cahagnes, south-west of Caen, during the advance towards Aunay-sur-Odon on 2 August 1944. The formation badge of 7th Armoured Division, which can be seen on the shoulders of two of the MPs in the centre of the photograph, suggests that these vehicles belong to 65th Anti-Tank Regiment. Note the exhaust cover on the nearest vehicle which is markedly different to those shown in the photograph at the bottom of page 11. The nearest Achilles is also depicted in the Camouflage & Markings section on page 21.

ANTI-TANK REGIMENT, ARMOURED DIVISION. JULY 1944

The three armoured divisions of British 2nd Army were all officially organised as shown here with two towed batteries, a battery of M10 3" tank destroyers and a battery of self-propelled 17pdr Achilles. Once again, the exact organisation varied and our diagram depicts 65th Anti-Tank Regiment of 7th Armoured Division. Note that a number of 6pdr guns were probably still on hand with the towed batteries when the division arrived in France. The individual batteries and the equipment of the anti-tank regiments of Guards Armoured Division and 11th Armoured Division are discussed in the main text.

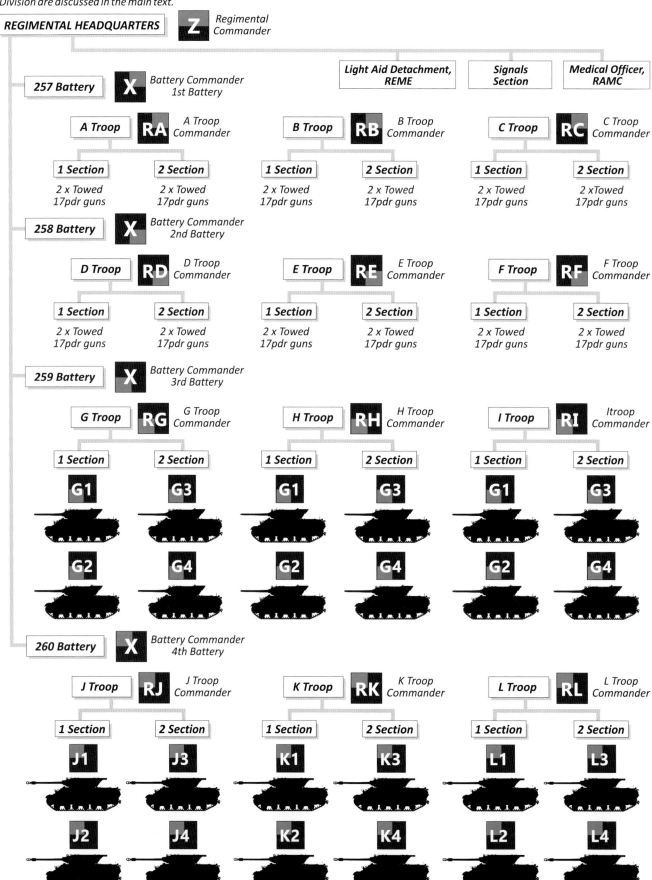

Full-colour versions of the tactical signs used by the Royal Artillery are shown in the Camouflage & Markings section of this book which begins on page 17.

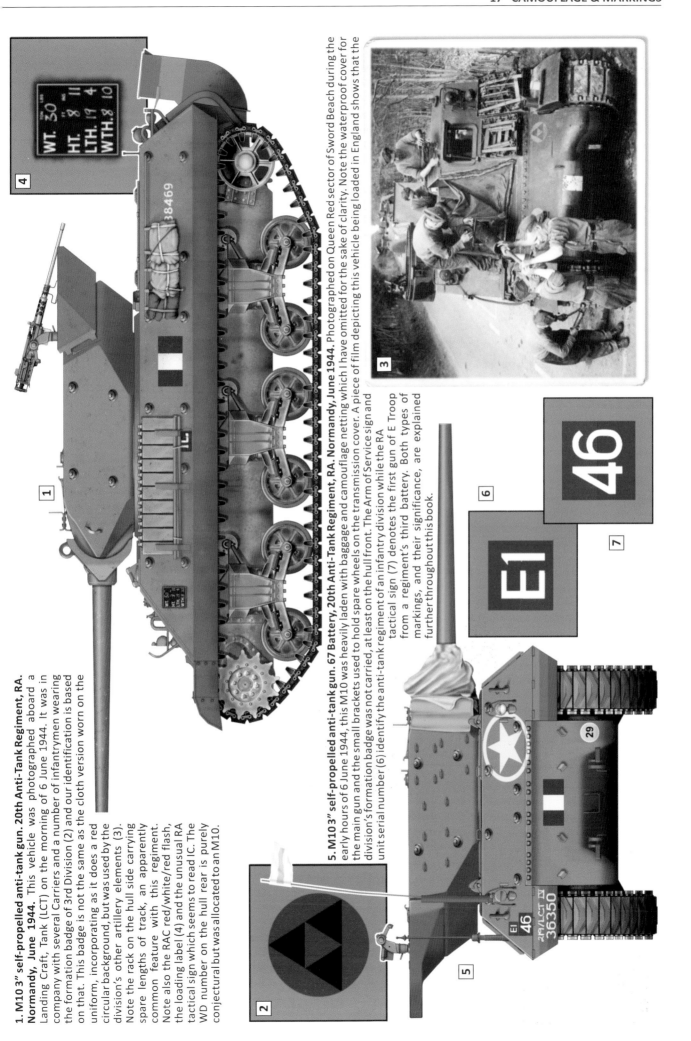

1. M10 3" self-propelled anti-tank gun. 20th Anti-Tank Regiment, RA. Normandy, June 1944. This vehicle was photographed aboard a Landing Craft, Tank (LCT) on the morning of 6 June 1944. It was in company with several Carriers and a number of infantrymen wearing the formation badge of 3rd Division (2) and our identification is based on that. This badge is not the same as the cloth version worn on the uniform, incorporating as it does a red circular background, but was used by the division's other artillery elements (3). Note the rack on the hull side carrying spare lengths of track, an apparently common feature with this regiment. Note also the RAC red/white/red flash, the loading label (4) and the unusual RA tactical sign which seems to read IC. The WD number on the hull rear is purely conjectural but was allocated to an M10.

5. M10 3" self-propelled anti-tank gun. 67 Battery, 20th Anti-Tank Regiment, RA. Normandy, June 1944. Photographed on Queen Red sector of Sword Beach during the early hours of 6 June 1944, this M10 was heavily laden with baggage and camouflage netting which I have omitted for the sake of clarity. Note the waterproof cover for the main gun and the small brackets used to hold spare wheels on the transmission cover. A piece of film depicting this vehicle being loaded in England shows that the division's formation badge was not carried, at least on the hull front. The Arm of Service sign and unit serial number (6) identify the anti-tank regiment of an infantry division while the RA tactical sign (7) denotes the first gun of E Troop from a regiment's third battery. Both types of markings, and their significance, are explained further throughout this book.

1. M10 17pdr self-propelled anti-tank gun. 65th Anti-Tank Regiment, RA. Normandy, June 1944. The units of 7th Armoured Division (2) were something of a law unto themselves in regard to vehicle markings, particularly during the division's time in the desert, and this Achilles provides a good example. I can, however, offer no explanation as to why I Troop should be included with the regiment's fourth battery (3) but the marking is quite clear in the photograph on which this illustration is based. Note the white undershading on the barrel of the main gun, another practice introduced during the North African campaign, and the Allied recognition star painted onto an ammunition box on the hull front (4). The WD number is completely speculative but was allocated to an Achilles.

4. M10 3" self-propelled anti-tank gun. Y Battery, 21st Anti-Tank Regiment, RA. Belgium, August 1944. This regiment was attached to the Guards Armoured Division (5) and the photograph on which our illustration is based was taken as the Guards entered Brussels. The name appears to correspond with the troop, in this case F, and there were numerous notations on the hull side in chalk, all illegible, probably made by the civilian population. Unfortunately the hull front was completely covered with stowage and camouflage netting obscuring any markings which may have been there.

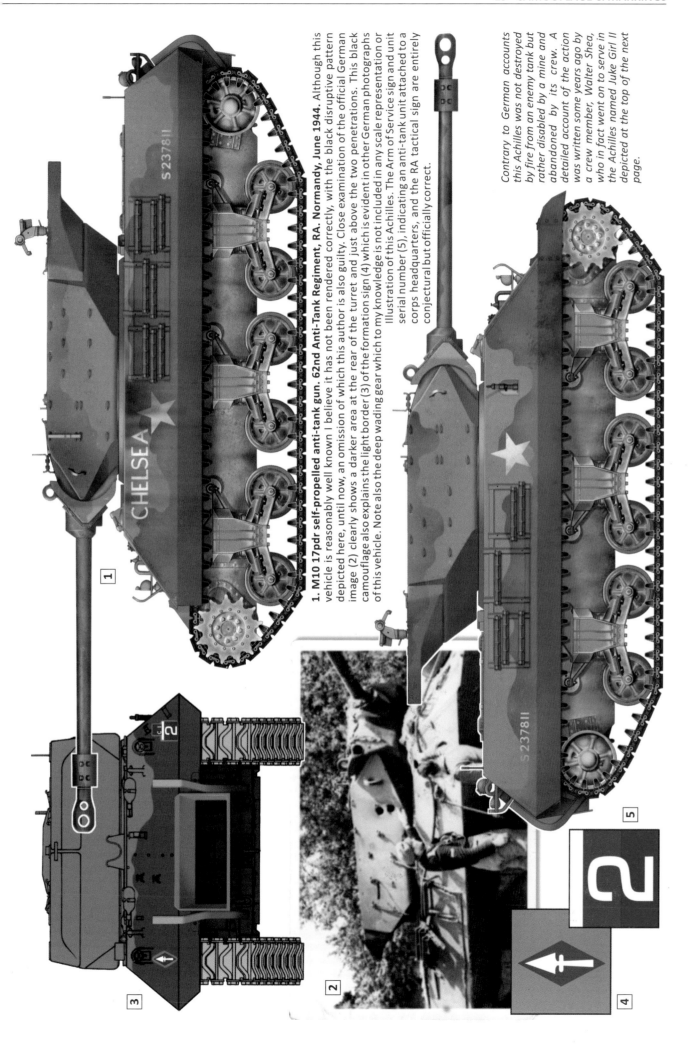

1. M10 17pdr self-propelled anti-tank gun. 62nd Anti-Tank Regiment, RA. Normandy, June 1944. Although this vehicle is reasonably well known I believe it has not been rendered correctly, with the black disruptive pattern depicted here, until now, an omission of which this author is also guilty. Close examination of the official German image (2) clearly shows a darker area at the rear of the turret and just above the two penetrations. This black camouflage also explains the light border (3) of the formation sign (4) which is evident in other German photographs of this vehicle. Note also the deep wading gear which to my knowledge is not included in any scale representation or illustration of this Achilles. The Arm of Service sign and unit serial number (5), indicating an anti-tank unit attached to a corps headquarters, and the RA tactical sign are entirely conjectural but officially correct.

Contrary to German accounts this Achilles was not destroyed by fire from an enemy tank but rather disabled by a mine and abandoned by its crew. A detailed account of the action was written some years ago by a crew member, Walter Shea, who in fact went on to serve in the Achilles named Juke Girl II depicted at the top of the next page.

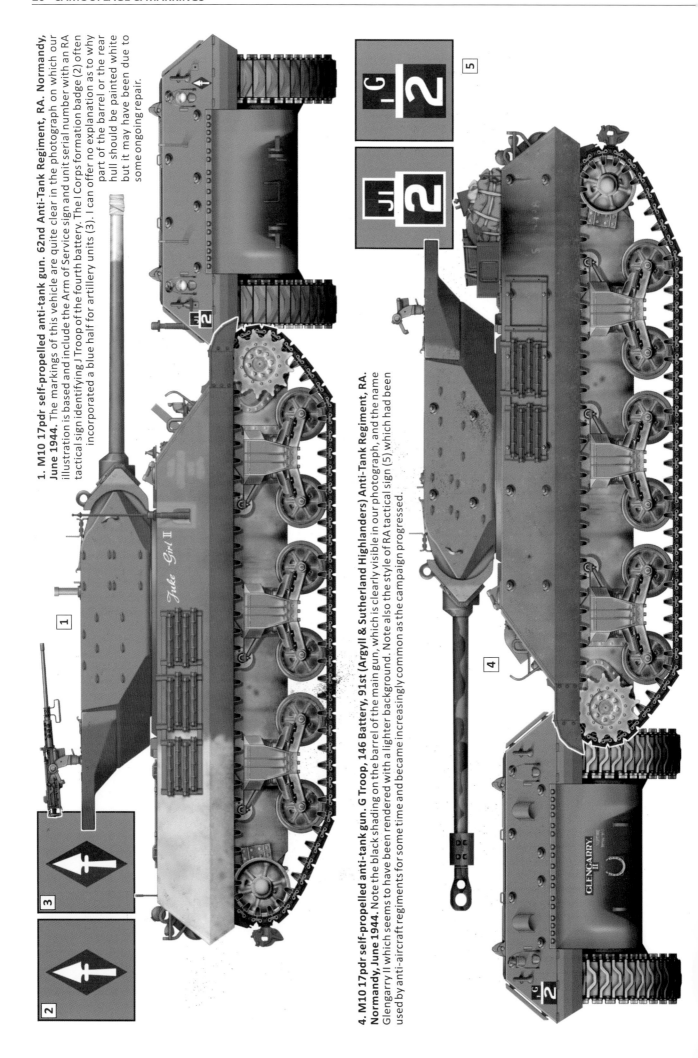

1. M10 17pdr self-propelled anti-tank gun. 62nd Anti-Tank Regiment, RA. Normandy, June 1944. The markings of this vehicle are quite clear in the photograph on which our illustration is based and include the Arm of Service sign and unit serial number with an RA tactical sign identifying J Troop of the fourth battery. The I Corps formation badge (2) often incorporated a blue half for artillery units (3). I can offer no explanation as to why part of the barrel or the rear hull should be painted white but it may have been due to some ongoing repair.

4. M10 17pdr self-propelled anti-tank gun. G Troop, 146 Battery, 91st (Argyll & Sutherland Highlanders) Anti-Tank Regiment, RA. Normandy, June 1944. Note the black shading on the barrel of the main gun, which is clearly visible in our photograph, and the name Glengarry II which seems to have been rendered with a lighter background. Note also the style of RA tactical sign (5) which had been used by anti-aircraft regiments for some time and became increasingly common as the campaign progressed.

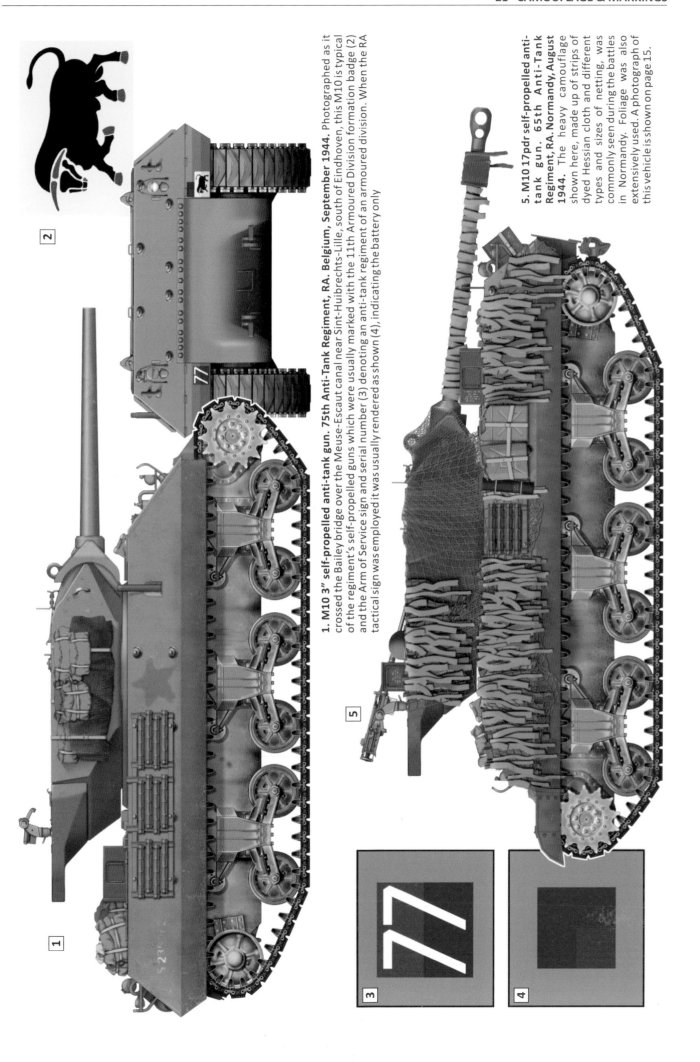

1. M10 3" self-propelled anti-tank gun. 75th Anti-Tank Regiment, RA. Belgium, September 1944. Photographed as it crossed the Bailey bridge over the Meuse-Escaut canal near Sint-Huibrechts-Lille, south of Eindhoven, this M10 is typical of the regiment's self-propelled guns which were usually marked with the 11th Armoured Division formation badge (2) and the Arm of Service sign and serial number (3) denoting an anti-tank regiment of an armoured division. When the RA tactical sign was employed it was usually rendered as shown (4), indicating the battery only

5. M10 17pdr self-propelled anti-tank gun. 65th Anti-Tank Regiment, RA. Normandy, August 1944. The heavy camouflage shown here, made up of strips of dyed Hessian cloth and different types and sizes of netting, was commonly seen during the battles in Normandy. Foliage was also extensively used. A photograph of this vehicle is shown on page 15.

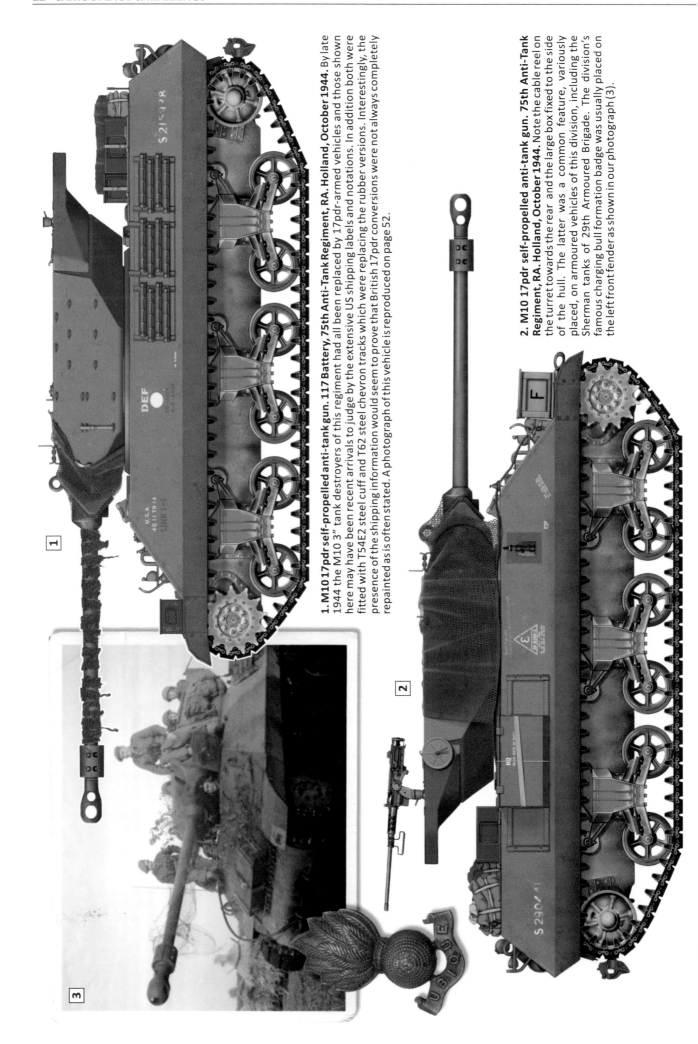

1. M10 17pdr self-propelled anti-tank gun. 117 Battery, 75th Anti-Tank Regiment, RA. Holland, October 1944. By late 1944 the M10 3" tank destroyers of this regiment had all been replaced by 17pdr-armed vehicles and those shown here may have been recent arrivals to judge by the extensive US shipping labels and notations. In addition both were fitted with T54E2 steel cuff and T62 steel chevron tracks which were replacing the rubber versions. Interestingly, the presence of the shipping information would seem to prove that British 17pdr conversions were not always completely repainted as is often stated. A photograph of this vehicle is reproduced on page 52.

2. M10 17pdr self-propelled anti-tank gun. 75th Anti-Tank Regiment, RA. Holland, October 1944. Note the cable reel on the turret towards the rear and the large box fixed to the side of the hull. The latter was a common feature, variously placed, on armoured vehicles of this division, including the Sherman tanks of 29th Armoured Brigade. The division's famous charging bull formation badge was usually placed on the left front fender as shown in our photograph (3).

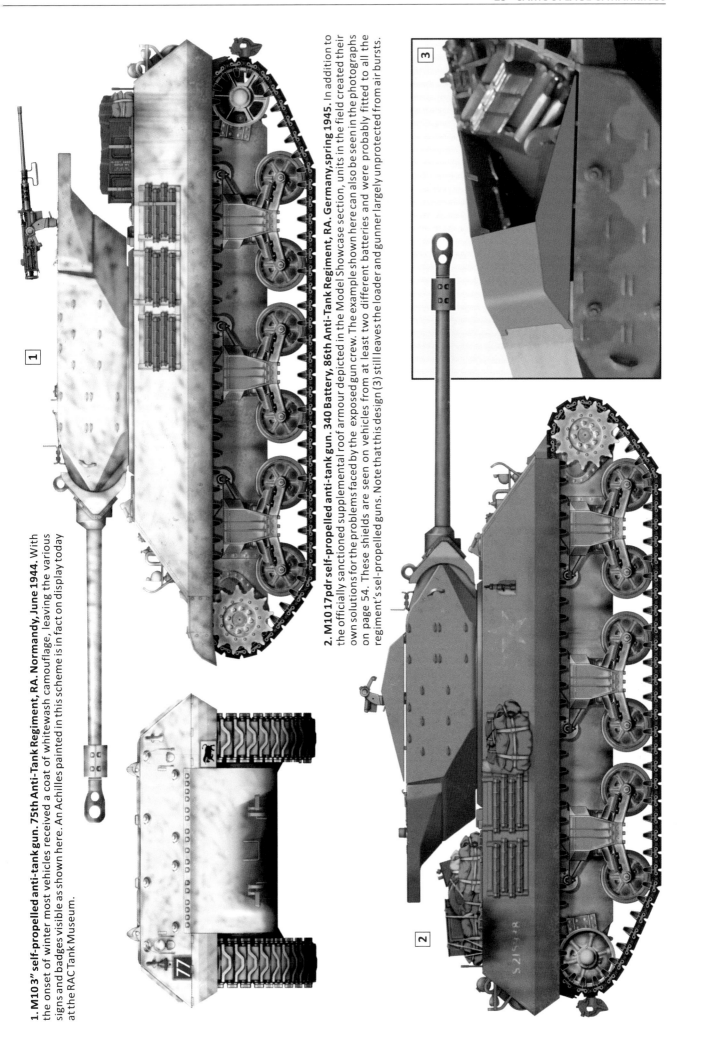

1. M10 3" self-propelled anti-tank gun. 75th Anti-Tank Regiment, RA. Normandy, June 1944. With the onset of winter most vehicles received a coat of whitewash camouflage, leaving the various signs and badges visible as shown here. An Achilles painted in this scheme is in fact on display today at the RAC Tank Museum.

2. M10 17pdr self-propelled anti-tank gun. 340 Battery, 86th Anti-Tank Regiment, RA. Germany, spring 1945. In addition to the officially sanctioned supplemental roof armour depicted in the Model Showcase section, units in the field created their own solutions for the problems faced by the exposed gun crew. The example shown here can also be seen in the photographs on page 54. These shields are seen on vehicles from at least two different batteries and were probably fitted to all the regiment's sel-propelled guns. Note that this design (3) still leaves the loader and gunner largely unprotected from air bursts.

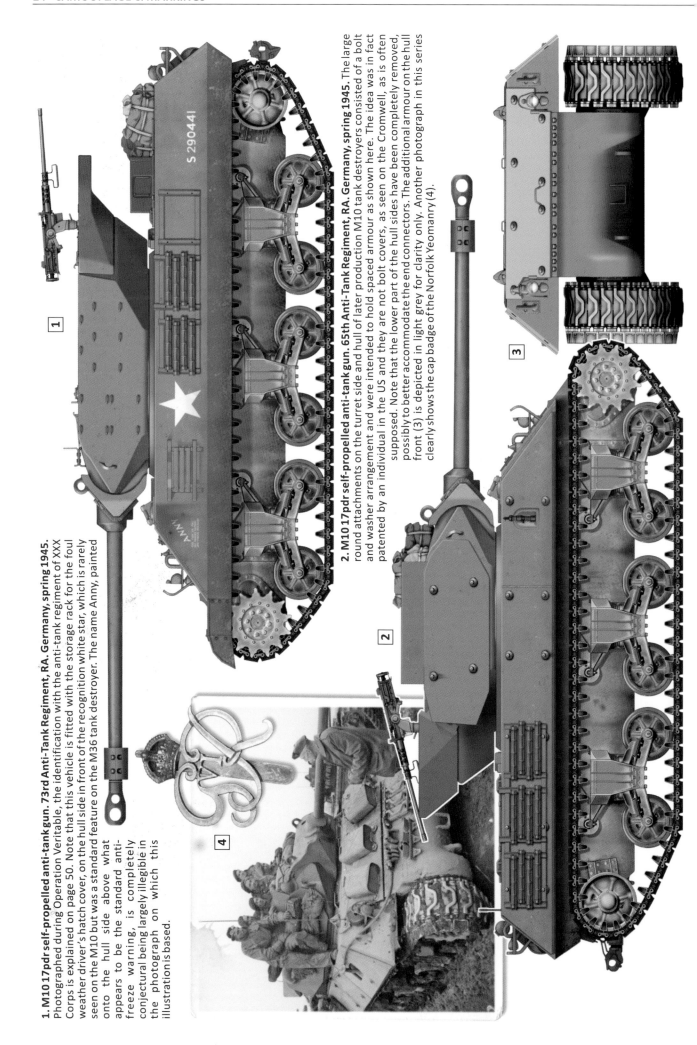

1. M10 17pdr self-propelled anti-tank gun. 73rd Anti-Tank Regiment, RA. Germany, spring 1945. Photographed during Operation Veritable, the identification with the anti-tank regiment of XXX Corps is explained on page 50. Note that this vehicle is fitted with the storage rack for the foul weather driver's hatch cover, on the hull side in front of the recognition white star, which is rarely seen on the M10 but was a standard feature on the M36 tank destroyer. The name Anny, painted onto the hull side above what appears to be the standard anti-freeze warning, is completely conjectural being largely illegible in the photograph on which this illustration is based.

2. M10 17pdr self-propelled anti-tank gun. 65th Anti-Tank Regiment, RA. Germany, spring 1945. The large round attachments on the turret side and hull of later production M10 tank destroyers consisted of a bolt and washer arrangement and were intended to hold spaced armour as shown here. The idea was in fact patented by an individual in the US and they are not bolt covers, as seen on the Cromwell, as is often supposed. Note that the lower part of the hull sides have been completely removed, possibly to better accommodate the end connectors. The additional armour on the hull front (3) is depicted in light grey for clarity only. Another photograph in this series clearly shows the cap badge of the Norfolk Yeomanry (4).

BRITISH ANTI-TANK REGIMENTS, NORTH-WESTERN EUROPE 1944-1945

In June 1944 the anti-tank regiments of the British Army were allocated to the various corps headquarters and to each of the infantry and armoured divisions of 21st Army Group. Each division also contained a number of field regiments, two in the case of an armoured division and three for an infantry formation, and a light anti-aircraft regiment. These, and the anti-tank regiment, were overseen by the division's Commander, Royal Artillery. Although the corps level troops were technically under the command of a counter bombardment officer their batteries were usually allocated to divisions as the need arose. Every attempt was made to provide the regiments of the Royal Artillery with a self-propelled element but many batteries were still equipped with towed guns when the war ended and the exact composition of each regiment is examined in more detail in the main text. Shown below are the Arm of Service signs, unit serial numbers and formation badges current at the time of the Normandy landings and for most of the North-west Europe campaign. Note that this does not include Canadian or Polish units which were also equipped with the M10 and Achilles.

21ST ARMY GROUP

21ST ARMY GROUP HEADQUARTERS

BRITISH 2ND ARMY

2ND ARMY HEADQUARTERS

Photographed near Tessel, south-west of Caen, in late June 1944 this jeep carries both the VIII Corps formation badge and an artillery Arm of Service sign with a white unit serial number identifying this regiment as 91st Anti-Tank Regiment. British units typically carried a full set of markings until late in the war when many seem to have been painted over.

Headquarters 21st Army Group controlled all the Commonwealth units serving in North-west Europe as well as the Polish, Belgian, Dutch and Czech contingents. Not shown here are the regiments of 1st Canadian Army which were also equipped with M10 and Achilles tank destroyers. British 2nd Army was directly subordinated to 21st Army Group and contained, in addition to numerous support elements, the formations shown below.

I CORPS

62ND ANTI-TANK REGIMENT, RA

VIII CORPS

91ST ANTI-TANK REGIMENT, RA

XII CORPS

86TH ANTI-TANK REGIMENT, RA

XXX CORPS

73RD ANTI-TANK REGIMENT, RA

3RD INFANTRY DIVISION

20TH ANTI-TANK REGIMENT, RA

5TH INFANTRY DIVISION

52ND ANTI-TANK REGIMENT, RA

15TH INFANTRY DIVISION

97TH ANTI-TANK REGIMENT, RA

43RD INFANTRY DIVISION

59TH ANTI-TANK REGIMENT, RA

49TH INFANTRY DIVISION

55TH ANTI-TANK REGIMENT, RA

50TH INFANTRY DIVISION

102ND ANTI-TANK REGIMENT, RA

51ST INFANTRY DIVISION

61ST ANTI-TANK REGIMENT, RA

52ND INFANTRY DIVISION

54TH ANTI-TANK REGIMENT, RA

53RD INFANTRY DIVISION

71ST ANTI-TANK REGIMENT, RA

59TH INFANTRY DIVISION

68TH ANTI-TANK REGIMENT, RA

GUARDS ARMOURED

21ST ANTI-TANK REGIMENT, RA

7TH ARMOURED DIVISION

65TH ANTI-TANK REGIMENT, RA

11TH ARMOURED DIVISION

75TH ANTI-TANK REGIMENT, RA

Shown below are additional samples of the Arm of Service and tactical signs employed by the units of the Royal Artillery. Note that most of these would not usually be seen on tank destroyers but they are included here to give the reader a broader understanding of what is a complex and at times confusing subject. From left to right: Corps headquarters; counter bombardment officer; Division headquarters; Commander RA, armoured or infantry division; Artillery regiment commander; Battery commander; Battery commander 102nd Anti-Tank Regiment. The Northumberland Hussars used their regimental colours until early 1945 at least and possibly later; Regimental signals officer. Units of the Royal Corps of Signals attached to artillery formations often, but not always, used the white and cobalt blue sign shown here.

M10 17PDR
ACHILLES

**21ST ANTI-TANK REGIMENT, RA
GUARDS ARMOURED DIVISION**

1/35 SCALE
RAMÓN SEGARRA

Spanish modeller Ramón Segarra's Achilles is based on the Italeri 1/35 scale kit and was built almost straight from the box. The images at the top of the page depict some of the interior detail, greatly enhanced by Ramón's expert painting and weathering.

The photograph below left shows the turret in its initial coats of paint and the breech of the 17pdr gun. At left is the fully-assembled hull with mask ready to have the black camouflage applied.

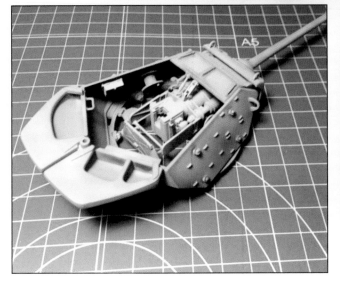

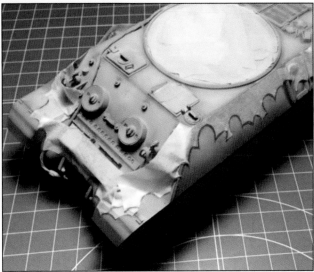

The completed Achilles after painting and extensive weathering. Ramón's model was built almost entirely straight from the box with some small added details such as the hand grip between the spare road wheels, made from plastic sheet, and the copper wire towing cable.

The markings depict a vehicle of 21th Anti-Tank Regiment of the Guards Armoured Division. As explained in the main text and Camouflage & Markings section, the SCC14 camouflage scheme, commonly referred to as Mickey Mouse, may have been far more common than is usually thought.

The stand-out feature of Ramón's model is the extensive yet subtle weathering, shown to good effect in the images above. The interior stowage, including the 17pdr rounds and ammunition cases, are part of the Italeri kit.

M10 17PDR
ACHILLES

75TH ANTI-TANK REGIMENT, RA
11TH ARMOURED DIVISION

1/48 SCALE
SATO MASANORI

Japanese modeller Sato Masanori's model is based on the Tamiya hull with the resin turret conversion set from Mr Modellbau. This vehicle is also finished in the so-called Mickey Mouse camouflage scheme made up of patches of Standard Camouflage Colour (SCC) 14 Black on SCC 15 Olive Drab.

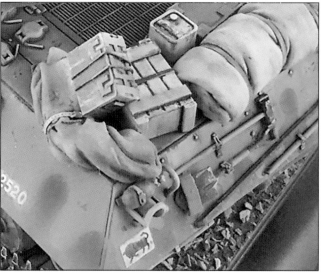

Masanori's model is finished in the markings of 11th Armoured Division and includes many extras such as the stowage and camouflage netting. The crewmen in their pixie suits are by Dartmoor Military Models, a British company that is perhaps better known for its extensive range of aircrew figures.

M10 3"
GUN MOTOR CARRIAGE

20TH ANTI-TANK REGIMENT, RA
3RD INFANTRY DIVISION
1/48 SCALE
SATO MASANORI

Masanori's model is based on the Tamiya 1/48 scale kit built from the box and painted in faded U.S. Olive Drab, as the great majority of these vehicles would have been. The base of this replica is particulary effective and Masanori used parts from the spares box and a stone wall in resin from Gasoline.

The crew member here is from Parabellum, a British company which manufactures a range of 1/48 scale figures. The resin stowage is from Black Dog, a Polish company which is featured regularly in this series.

M10 17PDR
ACHILLES

65 BATTERY
6TH ANTI-TANK REGIMENT, RCA
II CANADIAN CORPS

1/48 SCALE
LUCIANO RODRIGUEZ

44. M10 - 21 Army Gp Roof - View of No.1 in firing position for forward mounted .500 Browning.

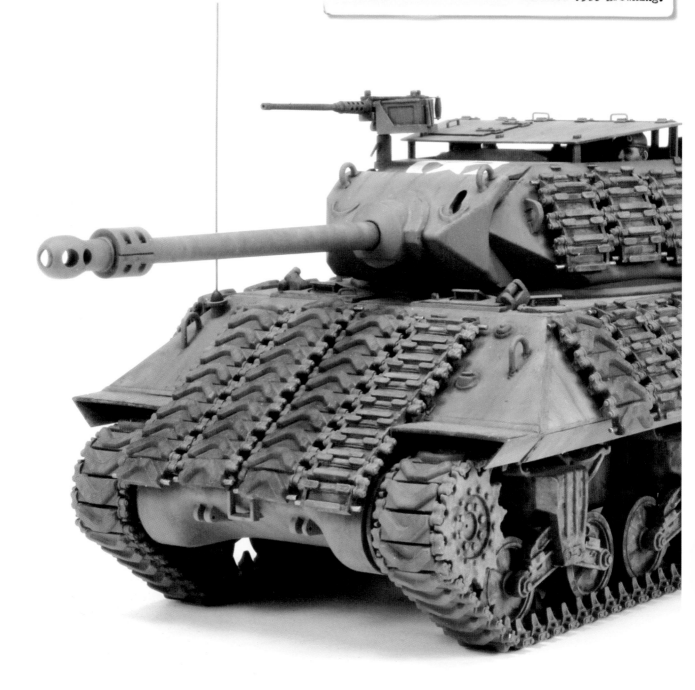

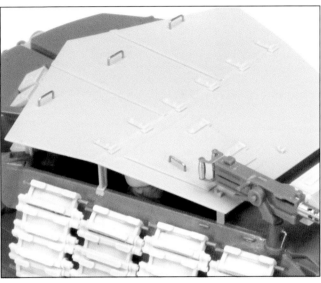

A number of units attempted to provide some form of overhead protection for the crews of the M10 and Achilles, and an example of this can be seen on page 23, but as far as is known only one official version was adopted by British and Commonwealth regiments. Luciano's model depicts one of these vehicles and is based on the wartime instructions and the accompanying plan drawings, part of which is reproduced in the photograph on the previous page.

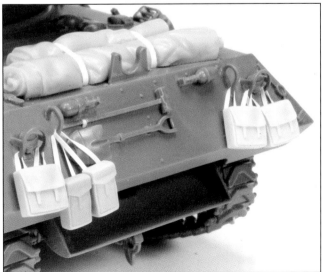

The armoured roof, with its forward-opening doors, handles and supports, was entirely scratchbuilt using the drawings that accompanied the official orders.

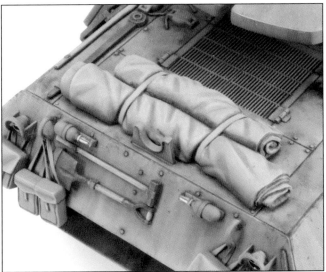

Luciano's model was built using the Tamiya 1/48 scale kit as a base with additional armour in the shape of Tamiya T48 rubber chevron and resin T49 steel cleat track links. The kit's 17pdr barrel was replaced with a metal conversion from RB Models while the crew figure and stowage were made from spare parts or scratchbuilt. Note that some of the tools have been moved from the hull rear plate to the rear deck and two British methyl bromide fire extinguishers have been added, all of which is correct for a British M10 or Achilles.

As many readers will be aware, the previous books in this series concentrated on the most popular modelling scales of 1/35 and 1/48 although I did endeavoured to include models in other scales where I could. In this project I tried to include as many smaller-scale versions as possible as these vehicles seem to be extremely popular with wargamers and small scale modellers.

In this book have deliberately chosen not to include information on aftermarket tracks as this was covered in both *Sherman Tanks: British Army and Royal Marines, Normandy Campaign 1944* and *Sherman Tanks: US Army, North-Western Europe, 1944-1945*. Also, I have not included a section on marking options as these seem to be limited, rather disappointingly, to two very well-known vehicles

which served in Normandy. In addition, I should mention that only products that would be appropriate for the British Army of the late war period are listed.

Due to reasons of space and the regular releases of new kits and accessories, this list is far from exhaustive and I would encourage readers to undertake their own research into the areas or variants that interest them most. An index of manufacturers can be found on page 64 of this book.

Note that although the names Achilles and Wolverine were in all probability never used during the war I have employed both here, as many manufacturers do, and throughout this book as a matter of convenience.

ACADEMY PLASTIC MODEL COMPANY

Based in Korea, this company's Military Miniatures range of 1/35 scale figures and vehicles includes an M10, first released in the 1970s and upgraded several times since then. The company's 1/35 scale Achilles was first offered in 2001 and although

some parts of the older M10 are utilised, many new features have been included. It has been called, in more than one review, an M10 with a 17pdr and accused of lacking many of the small details that were added by the British.

Below: Academy's 1/35 scale M10 built with photo-etched brass details by Tetra Model Works. Far right: Academy's 1/35 scale Achilles and one of the many boxes for the M10.

HOBBY MASTER LIMITED

This Hong Kong company produces a large range of die-cast military models in 1/72 scale. Although some are quite basic they are perfectly adequate for wargames armies and can of course be repainted. Although extra details can be added the die-cast metal is almost impossible to cut or even file and so

only the most basic conversions are possible. Many of the models seem to be based on larger Tamiya replicas. Shown below are, 1. The M10 in basic Olive Drab, 2. An M10 with roof armour and 3. An Achilles in the markings of a Canadian unit. The company also offers a range of aircraft.

TAMIYA INCORPORATED

This Japanese company has transformed itself from a post-war sawmill, which produced wooden models as a sideline, into the largest producer of scale model kits in the world.

The company's 1/35 scale M10 kit made its first appearance in 1975 but has been upgraded several times since then and a completely re-tooled kit was released in 2016. Just prior to that a 1/35 scale Achilles was on offer and this was subsequently upgraded when the new M10 kit was released. In 2003 Tamiya began releasing a series of models in 1/48 scale and this line has been extremely successful for the company, combining the potential for a high level of detail without the expense of the bigger kits. The 1/48 scale offerings include a mid-production version of the M10 and an Achilles. The latter is basically the M10 kit with the parts needed to build the 17pdr gun and a different set of markings.

Below: Tamiya's 1/48 scale M10 Mid Production kit. Right: The 1/48 scale Achilles in the markings of 62nd Anti-Tank Regiment. Note the applique armour on the hull glacis. This is not present in photographs of this vehicle.

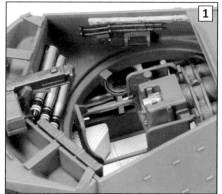

At left: Tamiya's M10 in 1/35 scale. This is the latest version of this kit, released in 2016 with new tooling and crew figures. Above, 1. The interior of the 1/35 scale Achilles turret. 2. Detail of the transmission cover and hull glacis of the 1/35 scale M10. 3. 1/35 scale drive sprocket, bogie and tracks.

AFV CLUB

Based in Taiwan, this company, a subsidiary of Hobby Fan, offers models of both the M10 and Achilles in 1/35 scale. AFV Club's M10 with mid production turret kit was first released in 1999 and has since been upgraded. All subsequent releases including the Achilles, M35 prime mover and M10 with late production turret, with the so-called duckbill counterweight, are based on the 1999 model. The company also produces workable track sets and British brass rivet sets.

Above: The AFV Club Achilles in its initial 2001 packaging. At left: The 1/35 scale M10 built with additional resin and copper details from Legend Productions, a South Korean firm specialising in scale model accessories.

ITALERI

This Italian company has been producing plastic models since its foundation in 1962. When the ESCI plastic model company ceased production Italeri were able to buy a number of the moulds and has continued to manufacture these kits under their own logo. The 1/35 scale Achilles kit, first released under the Italeri logo in 2010, is in fact a re-boxing of Academy's model which entered production almost ten years earlier. This kit is featured in the Model Showcase section from page 26. Italeri also offers a 1/56 scale model of the M10 designed to be compatible with 28mm wargames figures.

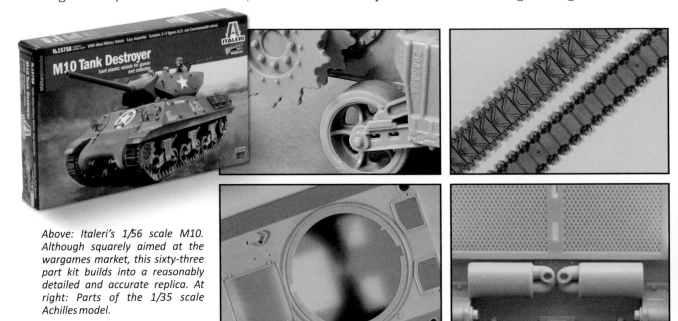

Above: Italeri's 1/56 scale M10. Although squarely aimed at the wargames market, this sixty-three part kit builds into a reasonably detailed and accurate replica. At right: Parts of the 1/35 scale Achilles model.

MILICAST AND DAN TAYLOR MODELWORKS

Founded in the 1970s and aimed squarely at wargamers, Milicast has steadily updated its range of resin cast models and today offers a Battlefield Series for its traditional customers and a Premier Range of more detailed kits. Shown below are the Achilles (1) and M10 (2). Formed in 2008, Dan Taylor Modelworks this company was founded by a former master model maker to Milicast and also

Accurate Armour and deals primarily in 1/76 scale with subjects related to the Normandy landings and the subsequent campaign including conversion sets, landing craft and large models such as a section of Mulberry Harbour. Shown here are Dan Taylor's water slide transfers applied to the Milicast M10 (3) and the massive Landing Craft, Tank (LCT) IV in 1/76 scale.

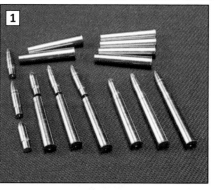

RB MODEL

RB Model from Poland produce a range of milled aluminium and brass gun barrels and resin accessories for 1/72, 1/48 and 1/35 scale armour models. Shown here are 1. 1/35 scale ammunition for the M10. 2. The muzzle brake, counterweight

and barrel of the 17pdr, also in 1/35 scale. 3. The breech of the same gun. 4. Live and spent rounds for the 17pdr. 5. A 1/48 scale 17pdr muzzle brake and barrel. 6. A barrel for the .30 cal machine gun also in 1/48 scale.

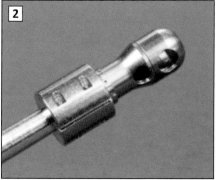

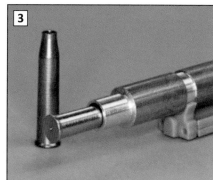

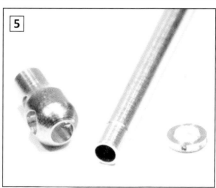

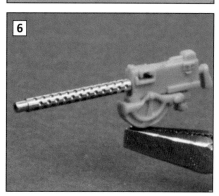

RUBICON MODELS

This is a relatively new company which produces a range of 1/56 scale tanks and armoured vehicles. The kits are obviously aimed at the wargaming market but are highly detailed and accurate, especially when compared to many other models manufactured in this scale. In addition, each model can be built as more than one variant. For example, the M10 kit comes complete with parts to build either the Achilles (1), two turrets for the American M36 or an M10 (2). The company also offers sets of waterslide transfers and has announced that crew figures will soon be available.

S & S MODELS

This British company produces a large range of complete vehicles and upgrade sets, predominantly in 1/72 scale although is a growing list in 1/56 and 1/100 scale. The latter are compatible with 28mm and 15mm wargames figures respectively. Made in resin and white metal, the models are primarily aimed at wargamers but they are reasonably well detailed and accurate. Shown below are accessories and crew figures for the 1/72 scale Armourfast Achilles

EDUARD MODEL ACCESSORIES

Founded in 1989 this Czech company produces high quality upgrade kits in photo-etched metal and resin and a number of scale models. The company's photo-etched brass detail sets for the Academy and AFV Club kits are currently out of production but can still be obtained from retailers. Shown below are parts of the upgrade set for the Academy 1/35 scale Achilles.

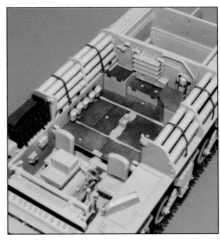

ABER

This Polish company has been manufacturing and selling upgrade sets since its foundation in 1995, working in photo-etched brass, milled aluminium and brass, stainless steel and even wood. For some time now Tamiya has included a number of Aber products with their model kits.

1. Aber's 1/35 scale upgrade set for the Academy M10 kit. 2. Part of the 1/48 scale detail set for the Tamiya M10. 3. The driver's periscope and headlight brushguards of the 1/35 scale set. Note that the holes cut away from the hull glacis have been made to show the interior detail and are not present on the unbuilt model. 4. Brass details for the .50 cal machine gun.

BLACK DOG

Based in the Czech Republic this company produces a large range of detailed resin accessory and upgrade sets for armoured vehicles in 1/35, 1/48 and 1/72 scale and a small number of complete kits. At present the company offers almost identical accessory sets in the three scales mentioned above. Shown below are, 1 and 2. 1/35 scale, 3 and 4. 1/48 scale, and 5 and 6. 1/72 scale.

ROYAL MODEL

This Italian company has been producing high quality accessories and aftermarket parts since the early 1990s under the guidance of its founder, Roberto Reale. The catalogue includes complete upgrade sets created specifically for the models offered by Dragon and Tamiya and also a number of generic items. Shown here are from 1 to 3. Parts in photo-etched metal and resin for the 1/35 scale M10 spplied to the Tamiya kit. 4 to 6. Details of the Academy 1/35 scale Achilles built with Royal Model's metal and resin details. Most of these parts could be used with other manufacturers models.

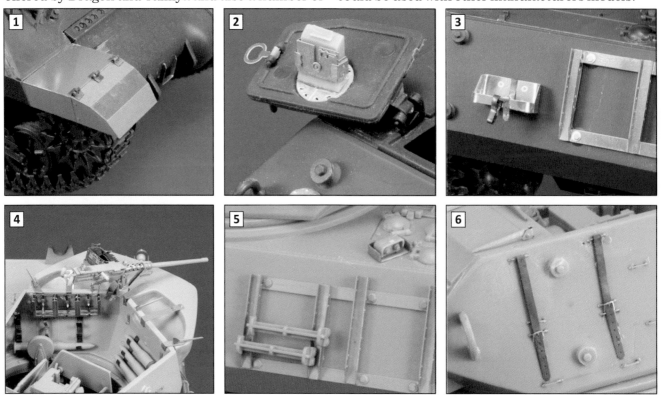

HAULER

Based in the Czech Republic, this company produces accessory sets in photo-etched brass and resin in 1/48, 1/35 and even 1/87 scale. At the time of writing the company's catalogue offered photo-etched sets for the M10 and Achilles in 1/48 scale and also for the 1/72 scale Armourfast model. The latter includes interior details for the turret which are totally lacking on the kit. Shown below is the upgrade set for the Tamiya 1/48 scale Achilles, including parts for the turret interior, and an armoured roof for the M10. The 1/48 scale Duckbill track extenders shown here are no longer in production although some retailers do have stock at the time of writing.

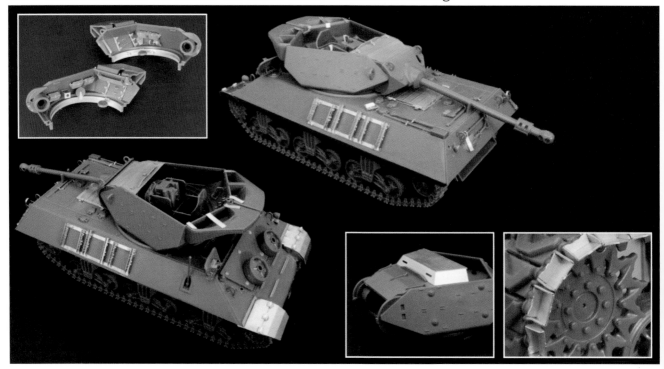

VOYAGER MODEL

Voyager have been manufacturing upgrade sets for scale models since 2003 with the release of their first set for 1/35 scale armour. The company produces two sets in photo-etched brass for the 1/35 scale M10 which can also be purchased as a single deluxe item. Shown below are parts from the basic set used to complete the AFV Club 1/35 scale kit.

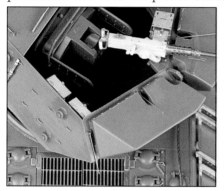  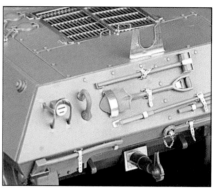

PASSION MODEL

This Japanese company produces a range of photo-etched detail sets, aluminium gun barrels, figures and water slide transfers to complement 1/35 scale models. In addition they act as a retailer for a number of manufacturers whose products are rarely seen in English-speaking countries such as Kamizukuri, Etokin Model, Swash Design and Raupen Modell.

Below: Passion Model's 1/35 scale detail set applied to the AFV Club M10. The various parts are made up of photo-etched brass, resin and nylon fibre. Note the casting marks on the gun mantlet and transmission cover

TETRA MODELWORKS

In the five years since its founding this Korean company has managed to create a large catalogue of photo-etched brass detail sets, mainly for aircraft and ships but also for scale armoured vehicles. Tetra offers two upgrade sets for the 1/35 scale M10, one marketed as being made specifically for the Tamiya kit and another for the Academy model. The latter incorporates a number of additional parts, most notably the engine access doors and fittings for a .30 cal machine gun.

E.T. MODEL

E.T. Model, a relatively new manufacturer from China, produce upgrade sets in 1/72 and 1/35 scale in brass and resin. The company's catalogue is heavily weighted towards modern tanks and German Second World War vehicles but there are a number of British and also US Army subjects. The company offers a photo-etched brass detail set for the M10 in 1/35 scale, details of which are shown below, which would be compatible with most of the available kits. Many of the external parts, such as tool clasps, grouser racks and periscopes would be of course be appropriate for the Achilles.

Above: An Achilles 17pdr self-propelled gun of 65th Anti-Tank Regiment photographed in Normandy during the summer battles. This vehicles is also shown and discussed in the Camouflage & Markings section on page 18. Below: Gunners of 65th (Norfolk Yeomanry) Anti-Tank Regiment photographed in Germany in February 1945, all wearing the so-called pixie suit. The cap badge, also shown at far left, is quite clear and I believe that at least two of these men are part of the crew depicted on page 24.

............text continued from page 14

Notes

1. As late as 27 January 1945 the commander of 279 Battery reported that his full strength consisted of D Troop with five 6pdr and E troop with four 17pdr guns.

66th Anti-Tank Regiment, RA (TA). Formed in 1939, the regiment was attached to 59th and 55th Infantry Divisions and remained in Britain for the duration of the war. Interestingly, it was at one time equipped with French 75mm guns.

68th Anti-Tank Regiment, RA (TA). Formed from parts of 58th Anti-Tank Regiment at the outbreak of war, by June 1944 this regiment, contained Batteries 269, 270, 271 and 272 and was attached to 59th (Staffordshire) Infantry Division. In August 1944 the division was disbanded and its men used as badly needed reinforcements.

70th Anti-Tank Regiment, RA (TA). Formed in 1939 from elements of 60th Anti-Tank Regiment, this unit was attached to 38th Infantry Division and remained in the United Kingdom for the duration of the war.

71st Anti-Tank Regiment, RA (Royal Welch Fusiliers). Formed from two batteries of 70th Anti-Tank Regiment in 1939 this unit contained 278, 279, 283 and 336 Batteries.

Attached to the 53rd (Welsh) Infantry Division, each battery was made up of one troop with 6pdr anti-tank guns and two troops equipped with towed 17pdr guns. The official history of the history of the Royal Welch Fusiliers published in 1960, titled *Red Dragon*, states that in August the batteries were reorganised with one of the towed 17pdr troops being re-equipped with 17pdr self-propelled guns. Worryingly, it goes on to describe the latter

as the Achilles, mounted on a Valentine chassis. The regiment's war diary mentions the support of a number of self-propelled troops from other units at this time, most notably 86th Anti-Tank Regiment, and this may have caused some confusion.

The first definitive entry regarding the regiment's own self-propelled guns is from 1 November 1944 when an officer and three gunners of 336 Battery were sent on a course to familiarise them with the new equipment, described as 'Valentine SP'. On 20 January 1945 the regiment's commander visited 336 Battery to watch the new vehicles in training but it was 5 February before all three troops had returned, fully equipped, to the battery. No mention is made of any allocation of self-propelled guns to the other batteries and it would seem that the regiment entered the fighting in the Reichswald and the subsequent advance into Germany with a single battery of Archers and three understrength towed batteries (1).

73rd Anti-Tank Regiment, RA (TA). Formed in November 1940 from elements of 13th and 52nd Anti-Tank Regiments, this unit consisted of 195, 196, 198 and 234 Batteries.

The regiment served in North Africa and returned to Britain in early 1944 where it was subordinated to XXX Corps headquarters. In June 1944 the regiment supported 50th Infantry Division during the D-Day landings and at that time 198 Battery was equipped with M10 tank destroyers while 234 Battery had three

............text continued on page 53

Said to have been photographed during Operation Veritable in early February 1945, these two Achilles self-propelled guns are following two of the newly-introduced Archer tank destroyers. Accounts which suggest that these vehicles are from 102nd Anti-Tank Regiment, which had relinquished all its M10 and Achilles well before this time, are certainly incorrect. What seems to be the formation badge of XXX Corps, shown at left, can just be seen on the rear of the second Achilles, making 73rd Anti-Tank Regiment a much more likely candidate. The vehicle in the foreground is also shown and discussed on page 24 of the Camouflage & Markings section.

ANTI-TANK REGIMENT, ARMOURED DIVISION, JANUARY 1945

By the end of 1944 many regiments had been in almost continuous combat since landing in Normandy and had also undergone organisational changes. The formation depicted here is 75th Anti-Tank Regiment of 11th Armoured Division just before the division was withdrawn from the front in February 1945. As can be seen from our diagram, the M10 tank destroyers with which the regiment began the campaign had all been replaced by Achilles 17pdr self-propelled mounts in Batteries 117 and 119. The towed batteries, were the majority of the regiment's casualties had been sustained, were temporarily converted to infantry companies. At about this time an unknown number of M22 Locust airborne tanks were received and allocated to the troop leaders. Photographic evidence would suggest that the Royal Artillery tactical signs were used by this regiment to indicate the battery only or, in most cases, not applied at all.

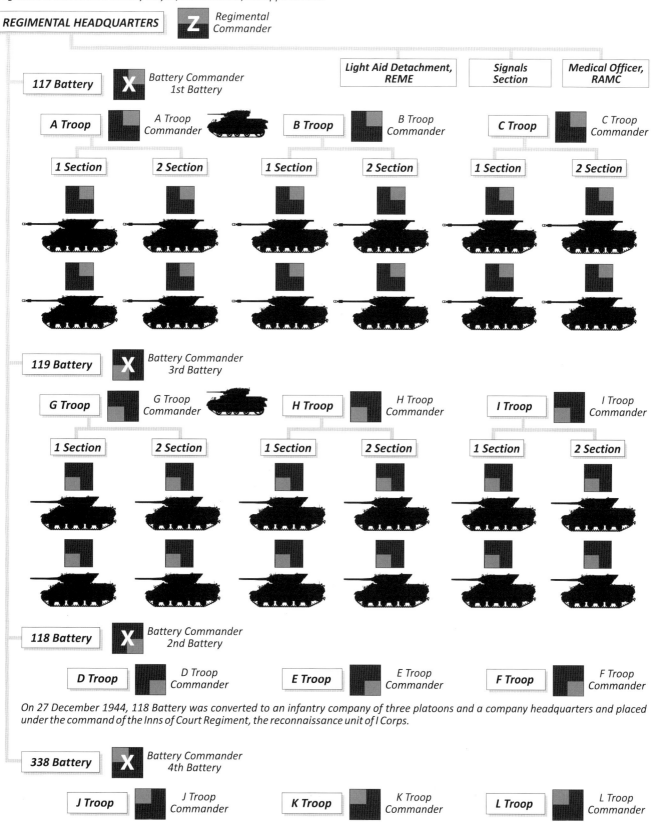

On 27 December 1944, 118 Battery was converted to an infantry company of three platoons and a company headquarters and placed under the command of the Inns of Court Regiment, the reconnaissance unit of I Corps.

On 25 December 1944, 338 Battery was converted to an infantry company of three platoons and a company headquarters, reinforcing the division's 159th Infantry Brigade.

Full-colour versions of the tactical signs used by the Royal Artillery are shown in the Camouflage & Markings section of this book which begins on page 17.

Photographed in Holland, close to the German border, on 12 October 1944 this Achilles of 75th Anti-Tank Regiment is said to have been the first British armoured vehicle to fire its main gun into German territory. Note the remains of the deep wading gear over the exhaust and, rather unusually for this time, a full set of track grousers on the hull side. The famous 11th Armoured Division formation badge can just be seen on the hull rear plate on the left-hand side.

Taken from the same series as the image reproduced on the following page, this photograph shows an officer of 117 Battery, 75th Anti-Tank Regiment atop one of the unit's Achilles tank destroyers in early October 1944 when the regiment was serving in the Netherlands. This picture is almost certainly posed as the drop leads to which the headset is connected are attached to the intercom box above the driver's position. The original US serial number and a full set of shipping details are the only visible markings This vehicle is also shown and discussed on page 22 of the Camouflage & Markings section.

...........text continued from page 50

troops of Achilles 17pdr self-propelled guns. These two batteries came ashore during the morning, the latter just 90 minutes after the first assault wave, and covered the eastern flank of 50th Division along the River Seulles.

Once the beaches were secured 195 and 196 Batteries, both equipped with towed 17pdr anti-tank guns, were able to land. The regiment took part in the battles in Normandy supporting 2nd Battalion, The Essex Regiment in the fighting around Tilly-sur-Seulles and 49th Division in the battle of Rauray which continued into early July 1944.

The regiment was involved in the final battles in Normandy and the subsequent pursuit of the German forces to the Belgian frontier, the so-called Great Swan, and in the battles in Holland.

75th Anti-Tank Regiment, RA (TA).

Formed in November 1940 from elements of 20th and 59th Anti-Tank Regiments, this unit was attached to 11th Armoured Division from 1941 until the end of the war.

Most of the division was ashore in Normandy by 13 June 1944 and at that time the regiment's 118 and 338 Batteries were each made up of three troops of towed 17pdr anti-tank guns while 117 and 338 Batteries were equipped with M10 tank destroyers and Achilles 17pdr self-propelled guns (1). From July 1944 the M10s were steadily replaced and by December both batteries were made up of three Achilles 17pdr troops receiving, in addition, a number of M22 Locust light tanks for the troop commanders. In the same month the towed batteries were used to form two infantry companies.

In February and March 1945 the regiment took part in Operation Veritable, the battle to clear the Reichswald, and the advance into Germany.

86th Anti-Tank Regiment, RA (TA).

Formed in November 1941 from the 5th Battalion, The Devonshire Regiment, this unit contained 128, 129, 130 and 340 Batteries. In June 1944 Batteries 128 and 130 were equipped with 17pdr anti-tank guns towed by Crusader tractors while the two remaining batteries were outfitted with M10 tank destroyers. There is some evidence that the regiment began to receive a number of Achilles self-propelled guns just prior to D-Day.

Subordinated to XII Corps headquarters, the regiment took part in the battles in Normandy, famously destroying five Tiger tanks and knocking down a Focke-Wulf fighter during the fighting for Hill 112. The regiment was involved in the engagements around the Falaise Pocket and the subsequent advance into eastern France and Belgium.

In November 86th Anti-Tank Regiment was transferred to the direct command of

Notes

1. I have not been able to determine with any certainty the exact composition of the self-propelled batteries at that time. In any case the M10s were soon replaced.

Photographed in October 1944 this Achilles self-propelled gun, like the vehicle shown on the previous page, retains a full set of US shipping markings on the hull. This proves that British 17pdr conversions were not always completely repainted in Standard Camouflage Colour (SCC) 2 as is often supposed. The British colour was very similar to US Olive Drab but did fade to a slightly greener shade. Note that both sets of tracks have been fitted backwards.

Above: An Achilles 17pdr self-propelled gun of 340 Battery, 86th Anti-Tank Regiment photographed during the Rhine crossing operations in March 1945. At right: An Achilles of 130 Battery, 86th Anti-Tank Regiment said to have been photographed in the Netherlands in November 1944. Note the name Glesca, for Glasgow, painted onto the transmission cover of the latter and the armoured shields on both. The vehicles of this regiment are also discussed on page 23 of the Camouflage & Markings section of this book.

2nd Army and took part in the Rhine crossing operations and the battles in western Germany. In February 1945 the Regiment's 129 and 340 Batteries were equipped throughout with Achilles self-propelled guns, which had presumably replaced all the M10 tank destroyers, and Sherman OP tanks.

88th Anti-Tank Regiment, RA (TA). Formed in November 1941 from the 2nd/9th Manchester Regiment, a Territorial Army duplicate of the 9th Battalion, this regiment was attached to 49th (West Riding) Division until July 1943.

The records are unclear on the regiment's next assignment but by January 1944, 88th Anti-Tank Regiment had been transferred to 45th (Holding) Division. In August 1944 the regiment left 45th Division to become 88th Training Regiment RA and was finally disbanded in 1947 having never left Britain.

89th Anti-Tank Regiment, RA (TA). Raised from the 2nd Battalion, Liverpool Scottish, a unit of the Territorial Army, in November 1942 the regiment was attached to 47th (London) Division. In October 1944 it was transferred to 55th (West Lancashire) Division to replace 66th Anti-Tank Regiment which had left the division in July. Before the end of the war this unit was converted into a light anti-aircraft regiment.

91st (Argyll & Sutherland Highlanders) Anti-Tank Regiment, RA (TA). Formed in November 1941 from 5th Battalion, The Argyll & Sutherland Highlanders (Princess Louise's), the regiment was under the command of VIII Corps headquarters until November 1944 when it was directly subordinated to 2nd Army.

The regiment contained 144, 145, 146 and 344 Batteries and in June 1944 two batteries were equipped with M10 tank destroyers while the remaining two were made up of three troops with towed 17pdr guns. Although it is uncertain how these were distributed it is known that 146 Battery was later equipped with Achilles 17pdr self-propelled guns and so it would be safe to assume that this was one of the earlier self-propelled batteries.

In his history of the Argyll & Sutherland Highlanders, Major Desmond Flower, who served with the regiment, states that Crusader AA tanks were used as OP vehicles. Crusader tractors were used to tow the regiment's 17pdrs and all vehicles were named for towns and villages of Scotland, some known examples being Drambuie, Dumfries, Dumbarton, Dundee, Dunoon and Duntocher.

After suffering heavily in the battles along the Maas in the Netherlands it was decided that the regiment would be disbanded on 1 January 1945 and replaced by 63rd Anti-Tank Regiment.

Photographed near Montcharivel, present-day Montchauvet, on 5 August 1944 this M10 tank destroyer seems to have no identifying markings but the insignia worn by the Lance Corporal, also shown below, almost certainly identifies this unit as 91st (Argyll & Sutherland Highlanders) Anti-Tank Regiment, which was at this time attached to VIII Corps. Of note is the pair of improved hook type 'Simplex' jacks, visible on the end connectors just below the drive sprocket, as well as the hinged front fender.

Photographed during the fighting in the Reichswald in February 1945 this Achilles is typical of the tank destroyers seen at this stage of the war with extensive camouflage, baggage and duckbill end connectors. Note that, once again, the grouser racks have been used as a means of carrying fuel containers and stowage. In the original image the cap badge of the Argyll & Sutherland Highlanders, shown above at left, is clearly visible on the headgear of the only crewman without an RAC helmet identifying this unit as 91st Anti-Tank Regiment.

Notes

1. Although it is quite impossible to determine colour from monochrome photographs the shades apparent on the tactical signs that are visible on the Archers seem to be identical to those used for the arm of service squares.

92nd (Gordon Highlanders) Anti-Tank Regiment, RA (TA). Formed from the 4th Battalion, Gordon Highlanders in November 1941, the regiment served with 54th Infantry Division, 9th Armoured Division and 61st Infantry Division in the United Kingdom.

94th Anti-Tank Regiment, RA (TA). Formed in 1941 from elements of the 22nd (Service) Battalion, The Royal Fusiliers, the regiment served with 76th and 80th Infantry Divisions until December 1944 when it was disbanded, having never left Britain.

96th Anti-Tank Regiment, RA (TA). Formed in July 1942 the regiment served with the Home Forces until the end of the war.

97th Anti-Tank Regiment, RA (TA). Formed in July 1942 by the amalgamation of 63rd (Worcestershire & Oxfordshire Yeomanry)and 64th (The Queen's Own Royal Glasgow Yeomanry) Anti-Tank Regiments and attached to 15th (Scottish) Infantry Division, the regiment contained 159, 161, 286 and 346 Batteries.

The regiment was equipped with 6pdr and 17pdr towed anti-tank guns throughout its service in North-west Europe and photo captions which identify M10 tank destroyers as belonging to this regiment are incorrect. Indeed, the regimental diary states that on 19 November 1944 three officers were temporarily transferred to VIII Corps headquarters to gain experience with self-propelled mountings, just ten days before the regiment was advised that it would be disbanded.

102nd (Northumberland Hussars) Anti-Tank Regiment, RA (TA). Formed in February 1940 from the Northumberland Hussars, a Yeomanry regiment, this unit was initially attached to 7th Armoured Division and later 50th Infantry Division seeing action in North Africa and Sicily before returning to Britain with the division in late 1943.

The regiment contained 99, 107, 288 and 289 Batteries and for the D-Day landings each battery was made up of two troops with 6pdr guns towed by Lloyd Carriers and a troop of M10 tank destroyers.

It was originally intended that the self-propelled guns would provide a degree of mobile fire support for the initial landings only and would be replaced at some later date by towed guns. However, they remained with the regiment until its transfer to 15th (Scottish) Division on 5 December 1944 when they were replaced by Archer 17pdr self-propelled guns.

In early March 1945 the two 6pdr troops of 99 Battery were converted to Archer self-propelled guns while the remaining batteries relinquished their 6pdr guns for towed 17pdr models. Uniquely this regiment used as system of dark blue and light blue RA tactical signs although photographic evidence would suggest that the normal red and blue signs were adopted for the Archers (1).

Men and vehicles of 11th Armoured Division, inlcuding a troop of Achilles tank destroyers and a Sherman VC Firefly, photographed in the village of St. Charles-de-Percy during the advance to Vire on 2 August 1944.

The organisation of the British Army of the Second World War period and the terms used to describe its various elements can be extremely confusing, particularly to the reader who may be approaching this subject for the first time. A detailed explanation of the notion of a regiment, the concept of seniority or precedence and the basic system of vehicle markings was included in the second book in this series *Sherman Tanks, British Army and Royal Marines, Normandy Campaign 1944* and it may be helpful to repeat parts of that here and also mention some aspects of the Royal Artillery. In 1939 the British Army was made up of a regular force of both full-time soldiers and reservists and the part-time volunteers of the Territorial Army which included the mounted regiments of the Yeomanry, some of which had been mechanised when the war began.

The Royal Regiment of Artillery. More commonly known as the Royal Artillery, or simply referred to in correspondence as RA, this is one of the oldest corps of the British Army. Artillery units have taken part in almost every major battle and campaign conducted by the army since 1346 when the first guns supported the English longbowmen at Crécy. Unlike the battalions of infantry and regiments of cavalry that are represented by flags and guidons, artillery units consider the guns themselves to be the regiment's colours and this explains the many instances where gunners fought bitterly to defend their weapons, destroying them as a last resort. Between the wars the artillery was made up of the Royal Horse Artillery (RHA), the Royal Field Artillery (RFA) and the Royal Garrison Artillery (RGA), as it had been during the 1941-18 war, with the addition of the Survey Battalion (1)

The artillery arm underwent a number of changes in 1938 when the brigades were renamed as regiments and the three-battery structure became standard (2).

At the same time, anti-tank regiments of infantry divisions were formed by converting and re-equipping five field regiments of the regular army and five field regiments of the Territorial Army (TA, see below). These regiments were each made up of four batteries and were outfitted with the 2pdr anti-tank gun. Just prior to the outbreak of war in September 1939, five infantry battalions of the Territorial Army were converted to anti-tank regiments and the number of TA artillery units was doubled, giving a total strength of 100 anti-tank batteries that had either been formed or were in the process of forming.

Although anti-tank units were organised as regiments the basic formation was the battery and these were numbered individually, the batteries of the Territorial Army being numbered in the 200 and upwards series. The exception to this were the batteries of the Royal Horse Artillery which were identified by a letter. Troops of anti-tank batteries were identified by a letter and these usually ran consecutively throughout the regiment but after the reorganisations of the early war years some batteries retained their original troop numbers when they were transferred to different regiments. An example of this is shown in the establishment of 20th Anti-Tank Regiment depicted on page 9 where 101 Battery contains troops M, N and O.

Notes

1. Prior to this survey and ranging, by sound and other means, had been the responsibility of the Royal Engineers.

2. This changed for field and horse artillery units in 1939 and again in 1940 with some artillery regiments of the BEF containing only two batteries. Heavy artillery regiments were different again but none of these need concern us here.

Photographed during the opening stages of Operation Goodwood on 18 July 1944, this Loyd Carrier of 21st Anti-tank Regiment has an Arm of Service square and RA tactical sign fabricated from thin metal sheet and rivetted to the front fender. The letters RG identify the commander of G Troop while 77 denotes an anti-tank regiment of an armoured division, in this case the Guards. The markings on the Sherman OP in the background indicate a troop commander of 55th Field Regiment, the division's senior artillery unit.

This Crusader Gun Tractor of 91st (Argyll & Sutherland Highlanders) Anti-Tank Regiment, with wading screens still in place, provides a very clear illustration of an artillery Arm of Service sign with the white bar denoting a unit attached to a corps headquarters. The white Unit Serial Number 2 identifies a corps level anti-tank unit while the RA tactical sign indicates the regiment's second battery. Note the unusual relief sculpture incorporating a thistle on the wading screen above the driver's visor.

Notes

1. Interestingly, this regiment was referred to as Royal Horse Artillery during its service in North Africa. The RHA title seems to have been dropped when the regiment returned to Britain in 1943.

2. Territorial battalions and Yeomanry regiments converted to regiments of the Royal Artillery were permitted to retain their titles and regimental distinctions, such as cap badges.

3. it should perhaps be remembered that these signs were intended to be indecipherable to the enemy and in many cases, particularly during the North African campaign, completely unofficial changes were introduced for specific battles without any detailed records being kept.

The Territorial Army. Originally formed in 1908 as the Territorial Force and renamed in 1921, this was basically a volunteer militia force reinforced by a number of regular army officers.

The Territorial Army, which included the Yeomanry regiments, had been greatly reduced following the First World War and hasty attempts to double the size of the force in early 1939 failed to make up for the lack of adequate support elements and training that characterised these units when the war began. By 1944, however, there was little difference between the Territorial battalions and those of the regular army.

The Yeomanry. These regiments were in fact the mounted component of the Territorial Army and by 1939 most had either been converted to a mechanised role, as part of the Royal Armoured Corps, or absorbed by the Royal Artillery. Anti-tank regiments raised from Territorial or Yeomanry units combined their former titles with their new regimental number, also adding the suffix TA. For example, 102nd (Northumberland Hussars) Anti-tank Regiment RA (TA) (1).

The Regiment. Although batteries could be transferred and even disbanded, Artillery regiments, like those of the cavalry, were more or less permanent formations, as they were in most European armies. In the study of the British army confusion sometimes arises in the case of infantry regiments which were essentially administrative and training organisations that raised battalions to be sent on active service. The battalions were numbered sequentially and retained the name of the regiment.

Precedence. The notion of precedence, more often referred to as seniority, is one of the pillars on which the British Army is built and the concept dates back to the time when the entire army would parade before the monarch with the most senior unit taking the place of honour on the right flank. In general terms, seniority is largely dependent upon when a regiment or battery was raised, with regular army formations taking precedence over Yeomanry and Territorial units (2).

Vehicle Markings. No other aspect of the British army of the Second World War period has generated as much consternation as the subject of vehicle markings. This is particularly true in the case of the system of Arm of Service (AoS) colours and Unit Serial Numbers. By 1944 the system had evolved into a complex yet manageable scheme that was, with exceptions, in use throughout the army. The most important markings un use during the North-west European campaign are listed below.

War Department (WD) Numbers. These numbers were an individual identifier issued for all vehicles, including trailers, by the War Office. Each number was prefixed by a letter describing the type of vehicle, S in the case of a self-propelled gun, and painted onto a suitable surface. The vehicle retained its WD number for the duration of its service life.

Bridge Classification Numbers. All British Army vehicles carried a sign indicating their weight class. The most common form this took was of a yellow circle with a black number indicating the vehicle's weight in tons although many variations in style and colour existed.

Recognition Markings. From July 1943 a large white star enclosed by a ring was introduced as an aerial recognition sign to replace the RAF-style roundel then in use. On tank destroyers this was usually modified to a white star without the ring, applied to the turret side, although the full version is encountered during the Normandy battles. The red/white/red Royal Armoured Corps flash introduced in early 1942 was rarely encountered by June 1944 but does seem to have been commonly employed by 20th Anti-Tank Regiment, at least for the D-Day landings.

Formation Badges. Officially all vehicles carried the badge of their higher formation, either a corps or division in the case of anti-tank regiments. Often incorporating intricate and colourful features, sizes, colours and designs examples are shown on page 25 of the Camouflage & Markings section.

Arm of Service Colours and Unit Serial Numbers. Sometimes referred to incorrectly as Arm of Service or AoS signs or squares, these coloured markings identified a regiment within a brigade or higher formation. Each sign was made up of a unit serial number painted in white onto a rectangle of the appropriate arm of service colour or colours (1). The addition of white bars indicated units which came under Army or Army Group command and examples are shown in the Camouflage & Markings section.

Royal Artillery Tactical Signs. In addition to the markings mentioned above artillery units could be identified by a system of coloured squares, approximately half the size of the Arm of Service signs, which denoted regimental headquarters and the individual batteries combined with a series of letters and numbers these tactical signs could identify each component of the regiment including the various support elements.

Camouflage Colours. All colours for use with vehicle camouflage and their application were stipulated in British Standard (BS) 381C of 1930 and BS 987C of 1942. The colours in use with the British Army at the time of the Normandy landings and in the subsequent campaign in North-western Europe were Standard Camouflage Colour (SCC 2) and Standard Camouflage Colour (SCC 15).

However, as the M10 tank destroyers were delivered directly from the United States it is only reasonable to assume that they were painted in US Army No.9 Olive Drab(2). The exception to this would have been the vehicles that were returned for extensive repairs or were converted to carry the 17pdr which would have necessitated at least some repainting of the turret and gun (3).

Standard Camouflage Colour (SCC 2). Sometimes referred to as brown, khaki brown or service drab and described as a rich, dark brown tending towards khaki. Although this colour was replaced in April 1944 by SCC 15 it could be seen for some time after that as paints were customarily used until stocks were exhausted.

Standard Camouflage Colour (SCC 15). Introduced in April 1944 this colour was referred to as Olive Drab and was very similar to the US Army colour of the same name, the major difference was that it tended to fade to a greener shade. Vehicles returned for extensive repairs would very probably have been repainted with SCC 15.

Notes

1. In the case of all artillery units this was red over blue.

2. Tanks and self-propelled guns received from the United States where painted in this colour and were not usually repainted unless absolutely necessary. It is almost certain that most M10 tank destroyers that were initially sent to France were painted in this colour. Vehicles returned for extensive repairs may well have been repainted with SCC 15 as would the 17pdr conversions.

3. The photographs on page 52 and page 53 clearly show US shipping markings meaning that the hulls of those vehicles could not have been repainted, although the turrets may have been.

In October 1943 a disruptive pattern of camouflage rendered in SCC 14 Black was authorised for vehicles painted in SCC 2 and this resulted in the so-called Mickey Mouse scheme camouflage commonly seen on lorries and other soft-skinned transport during the Normandy campaign. In April 1944 when SCC 15 was first introduced the new colour was only applied to the areas of SCC 2, leaving the disruptive pattern of SCC 14 Black visible. This scheme seems to have also been applied to some tracked vehicles and given that most of the photographic evidence we have depicts tanks and self-propelled guns which are covered in foliage, netting and stowage in addition to a heavy coat of dust and dirt, the practice may have been more widespread than is thought. At far right, a page from GS Publication 644 of 1941 explaining how disruptive camouflage patterns were to be applied.

Although the US Army's tank destroyer battalions went into combat equipped with the M3 75mm and M6 37mm Gun Motor Carriages, as mentioned in the Introduction, it soon became obvious that crew protection was almost as important as mobility and firepower. Experiments with an open-topped M3 medium tank and an M4A2 Sherman with a re-designed turret, designated T24 and M35 respectively, proved unsatisfactory and although both went through a number of design changes and emerged as the M9 and T35, neither were accepted for production. However, the T24 and M35 had highlighted the benefit of mounting a powerful gun on an armoured, fully-tracked chassis and all future development would follow these lines. Another design, the T35E1, was a further development of the T35 which was also based on the chassis of the diesel-powered M4A2 but featured a completely new hull made up of sloped armour plates. To maintain the protection offered by the sloped armour, the driver's hoods and hull machine gun, identical to those fitted to the Sherman, were dropped from the design. The turret, while similar in appearance to the T35, was made from rolled steel plates as opposed to the cast turret of the earlier model. In June 1942 the new design was approved for production and designated 3" Gun Motor Carriage (GMC) M10. The turret, as it was originally envisaged, was made up of six sides and a gun shield but was replaced by a pentagonal version before production commenced. The turret of the M10 was designed to enable the 3" gun to be replaced, if required, by the 105mm howitzer and although this conversion was never carried out, it proved to be a fortuitous decision as the British 17pdr anti-tank gun could be fitted to the production turret with very little effort. Assembly was carried out by the Fisher Body Plant, a division of General Motors, from September 1942 until December 1943 by which time a total of 4,993 M10 tank destroyers had been completed. A similar vehicle, the M10A1, was produced by Ford but as none of the 1,413 completed assemblies ever left the US, we can ignore them here.

Notes

1. As a matter of interest a Mr Quentin Berg, one of the designers of the M10, filed a patent for this arrangement in May 1943.
2. In many American publications these are referred to as mid-production turrets. The first counterweights, which resembled two large boxes weighing approximately 2,400 pounds, were not fitted to vehicles sent to Britain. The Duckbill design was introduced to replace the Fisher counterweights which, at 3,700 pounds, were found to be too heavy.

The M10 Turret. The complexities of the original design for the turret of the T35E1, which was hexagonal in shape with a large gun shield, had not been dealt with when the M10 was finally accepted for production and an interim pentagonal version was proposed. By the time the problems with the hexagonal model were solved, assembly jigs and fixtures for the five-sided turret had been acquired and it was decided to continue production with the new design (A). The partial roof was also reduced and the turret periscopes of the initial specification were dropped. The heavy gun shield (B) was 70mm thick while the turret sides were of 25mm thickness. Additional armour protection, in the shape of armour plates, could be fitted to the turret sides and held in place by means of four large bolts which were fastened to steel bosses (C) welded to the turret (1). Provision was also made to attach additional armour to the hull by the same means (D) but it seems that the armour plates were rarely, if ever, issued. However, locally-produced versions were certainly manufactured by British units at least and an example can be seen on page 24 of the Camouflage & Markings section of this book. A very early modification was the addition of fourteen small brackets (E), welded to the turret sides. Canvas or leather straps were threaded through these to hold the tarpaulins, blankets and other baggage.

It soon became clear that the turret traverse was hampered by the weight of the 3" gun, particularly on sloping ground, and in an effort to correct the balance a number of track grousers were attached to the turret rear. This proved to be less than satisfactory and in January 1943 a wedge-shaped counterweight (F), designed by Fisher, was welded to the rear of the turret. These earlier model turrets with their distinctive counterweights were referred to by the British as the V Type (2).

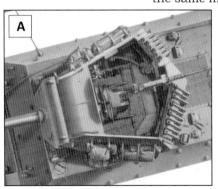

In March 1943 a new turret design was introduced into production with a less angled rear plate, which gave the crew slightly more room while the re-designed 2,500-pound counterweight which was known, almost universally, as the Duckbill Type replaced the Fisher version (A). Shortly after this the steel bosses and bolts were dropped from production although it appears that the small brackets were retained.

The turret was capable of traversing through 360 degrees but its operation was completely manual and this proved to be a disadvantage.

The 17pdr conversion. Although fitting the OQF 17pdr to the M10 turret presented far fewer problems than it had with the M4 Sherman, the barrel was slightly smaller than the standard 3" gun and so an armoured collar (B) was welded to the M10 gun shield. This collar, and the large two-piece counterweight attached to the barrel, helped to offset the problems with balance caused by the heavy 17pdr breech. A bump stop was welded onto the turret roof behind the gun shield reducing the maximum elevation to 20 degrees and a hole was cut through the gun shield on the left-hand side to accommodate the direct sight telescope (C).

New ammunition racks were installed to hold the 17pdr ammunition with six rounds carried in the turret and a further forty-four stored in the hull sponsons. Other peculiarly British inclusions to the turret interior were four Sten guns and a number of hand grenades held in boxes, a binocular case, a hand-held rangefinder, map boards, signal flags and a methyl

bromide fire extinguisher. A number of accounts state that these 17pdr conversions were referred to as Achilles IC and Achilles IIC, describing vehicles with the earlier and later turrets respectively (1). While I have been unable to either confirm or deny this I should mention that in all the regimental diaries and combat reports that I have been able to examine while preparing this book I have not found a single instance of the use of the word Achilles. Nor is it employed in the official stowage instructions, issued in May 1944, where the turrets are in fact referred to as V Type and Duckbill Type

The M10 Hull. As the tank destroyer concept emphasised speed and firepower, the armour of the M10 was relatively thin in comparison to the M4 series of medium tanks, with the exception of the lower hull which was essentially a modified M4A2 (2).

Reports from the early battles in the Philippines, which were taking place during the design phase, had emphasised the value of sloped armour and the 19mm thick hull sides and rear plate of the T35E1 were angled at 38 degrees to the vertical and 12.7mm skirts, which sloped inwards, were fitted along the lower edge of the sponsons (D). In the field, these skirts could inhibit the use of extended end connectors and were sometimes removed, together with the front fenders. The three-piece bolted transmission cover of the prototype T35E1 was replaced in production by the cast version with the rounded type (E) fitted to the first vehicles, later replaced by the so-called sharp-nose type (F) (3).

Notes

1. The suffix C was indeed applied to the 17pdr Sherman conversions, for example Sherman VC.

2. The M10A1 was based on the petrol-engined M4A3.

3. It is thought that the sharp-nose transmission covers were introduced by Fisher into the M4A2 assembly in July 1943 but an exact date for the M10 is unknown.

In both cases the armour of the transmission cover was just over 50mm thickness. A step was welded to the centre of the cover (A) and metal strips were welded to each of the front towing lugs.

The driver and assistant driver were provided with outward opening hatches, each fitted with a single M6 periscope (B). The hull glacis plate was 38mm thick and sloped at 55 degrees to the vertical. The headlights and brush guards were those used on the M4A2.

Provision for additional armour was provided by the same steel boss and bolt arrangement described for the turret with twelve fixed to each side of the hull and eight on the glacis.

When counterweights were incorporated into production the grousers were moved from the turret rear to the hull sides and were held on a metal rack which could be attached to the steel bosses. When the latter were dropped from production the racks were simply welded to the hull (C).

In production vehicles the pioneer and maintenance tools were carried on the hull rear plate but some of these were moved to the rear deck by the British as described in the following paragraphs.

British modifications to the M10 hull.
Two brackets were welded to the transmission cover to hold six spare tracks. An aerial for the A set, No. 19 wireless was fitted to the glacis on the right side behind the headlight. The aerial for the B set was placed in the indentation on the hull right hand side. The towing cable, shovel, sledgehammer and mattock head were retained but the axe, crowbar, mattock handle and track adjusting tool were moved to the rear deck. Two standard methyl bromide fire extinguishers were held in brackets on the rear plate next to the lifting eyes and a box for a small first aid kit was fixed to the rear deck on the left hand side corner.

Photographic evidence shows that on some vehicles, contrary to official instructions, the crowbar was left in place and it is possible that other small alterations were neglected. British units in the field carried out their own modifications to both the M10 and the 17pdr conversion including the fabrication of turret roof armour, fitting additional wireless aerials and applique armour for the turret and hull and examples of these are shown in the Camouflage & Markings section.

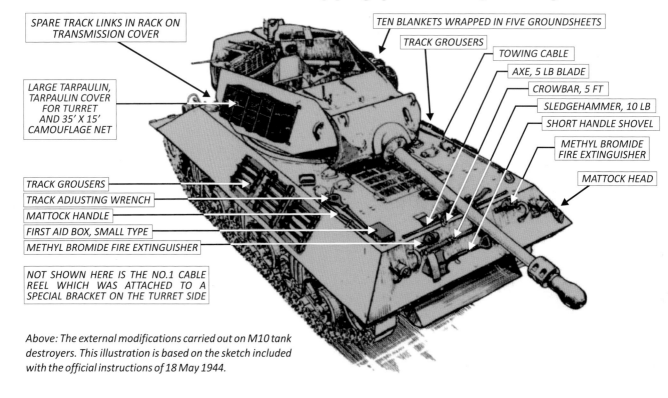

SPARE TRACK LINKS IN RACK ON TRANSMISSION COVER

LARGE TARPAULIN, TARPAULIN COVER FOR TURRET AND 35' X 15' CAMOUFLAGE NET

TRACK GROUSERS

TRACK ADJUSTING WRENCH

MATTOCK HANDLE

FIRST AID BOX, SMALL TYPE

METHYL BROMIDE FIRE EXTINGUISHER

NOT SHOWN HERE IS THE NO.1 CABLE REEL WHICH WAS ATTACHED TO A SPECIAL BRACKET ON THE TURRET SIDE

TEN BLANKETS WRAPPED IN FIVE GROUNDSHEETS

TRACK GROUSERS

TOWING CABLE

AXE, 5 LB BLADE

CROWBAR, 5 FT

SLEDGEHAMMER, 10 LB

SHORT HANDLE SHOVEL

METHYL BROMIDE FIRE EXTINGUISHER

MATTOCK HEAD

Above: The external modifications carried out on M10 tank destroyers. This illustration is based on the sketch included with the official instructions of 18 May 1944.

Suspension, wheels and tracks. The lower hull of the M10, including the running gear and tracks, was essentially the same as the M4A2 tank. As Fisher Body was the main producer of the M4A2, and the sole manufacturer of the M10, it seems likely that the component parts used in the assembly of the latter closely resembled those of the tank.

The suspension was made up of two drive sprockets, six bogie assemblies with two roadwheels, a large roller and track skid and a rear idler. All these parts went through numerous changes during the production of the M4 medium tank and many are described in other books in this series notably *Sherman Tanks: British Army and Royal Marines, Normandy Campaign 1944* and *Sherman Tanks: US Army, North-western Europe 1944-1945.*

Shown below are examples of the various elements of the M10 suspension.

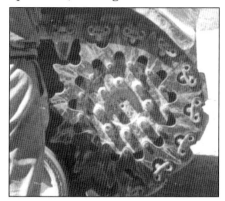

Above, left to right: The 13-tooth drive sprocket cut from a metal plate. These seem to be more commonly seen on vehicles with the earlier turret. The simpler drive sprocket, also cut from plate. Photographs would suggest that these were more often fitted to vehicles with the later style turret and may therefore have replaced the more complex version. The pressed steel rear idler. A spoked version was also commonly seen on Sherman tanks until the end of the war but this version seems to have been most often fitted to the M10.

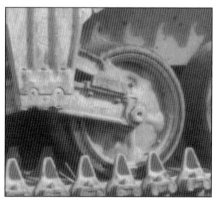

Above, left to right: Common M10 track types. T41 Rubber Block Tracks. Featuring a flat, reversible rubber tread, production of these tracks was discontinued in mid-1943 but many are seen in use late in the war. T48 Rubber Chevron Tracks fitted with extended end connectors. These tracks were popular with crews and a version remained in production in the post-war years. T54E2 Cuff Design Tracks. This was one of the first steel chevron type tracks to go into service. Other track types such as the T54E1 and T62 types are seen on British M10 and Achilles tank destroyers and these are shown in some of the photographs in the main text.

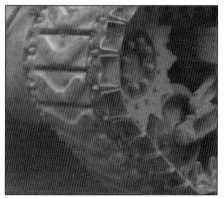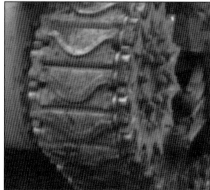

Above, left to right: Common M10 track types. T41 Rubber Block Tracks. Featuring a flat, reversible rubber tread, production of these tracks was discontinued in mid-1943 but many are seen in use late in the war. T48 Rubber Chevron Tracks fitted with extended end connectors. The end connecters were produced in several different, but similar, configurations and could add several inches to the width of the track. In some case the armoured skirt of the lower hull was completely removed to allow the extended connectors to be fitted. These tracks were popular with crews and a version remained in production in the post-war years. T54E2 Cuff Design Tracks. This was one of the first steel chevron type tracks to go into service. During the extremely cold winter of 1944-5 it was found that these, and other steel tracks, were liable to lose traction on the ice-covered roads and a number of anti-tank regiment unit diaries mention that requests were made to replace the steel tracks with rubber versions. Other track types such as the T54E1 and T62 types are seen on British M10 and Achilles tank destroyers and these are shown in some of the photographs in the main text.

Tamiya Inc
Shizuoka City, Japan
www.tamiya.com

Academy Plastic Model Company
Yonghyeon-dong, Uijeongbu-Si,
Gyeonggi-Do, Korea
www.academy.co.kr

Royal Model
Via E. Montale, 19-95030 Pedara, Italy
www.royalmodel.com

Italeri S.p.A.
via Pradazzo 6/b
40012 Calderara di Reno, Bologna, Italy
www.italeri.com

Resicast
517 Vieux Chemin de Binche,
7000 Mons, Belgium
www.resicast.com

Accurate Armour
Kelburn Business Park, Port Glasgow Pa14
6TD, United Kingdom
www.accurate-armour.com

Eduard Model Accessories
Mirova 170, 435 21 Obrnice,
Czech Republic
www.eduard.com

Rubicon Models
www.rubiconmodels.com

Dan Taylor Modelworks
55 Town Hill,
West Malling, Kent, ME19 6QL,
United Kingdom
www.dantaylormodelworks.com

Hauler
Moravská 38, 620 00 Brno,
Czech Republic
www.hauler.cz

Voyager
Room 501, No.411 4th Village
SPC Jinshan District, Shanghai 200540,
China
www.voyagermodel.com

Aber
ul. Jalowcowa 15, 40-750 Katowice,
Poland
www.aber.net.pl

E.T. Model
www.etmodeller.com

Friulmodel
H 8142. Urhida, Nefelejcs u. 2.,
Hungary
www.friulmodel.hu

Modelkasten
Chiyoda-ku Kanda, Nishiki-Cho 1-7, Tokyo,
Japan
www.modelkasten.com
Very difficult to navigate but worthwhile

Black Dog
Petr Polanka
Letecká 549, Libèice nad Vltavou,
252 66, Czech Republic
www.blackdog.cz

Milicast Models
9 Rannoch St., Battlefield,
Glasgow G44 4DF, United Kingdom
Tel: 0141 633 1400
www.milicast.com

RB Model
Powstancow Wlkp.29B,
64-360 Zbaszyn,
Poland
www.rbmodel.com

Passion Models
www.passionmodels.jp

Kaizen
Available from Hobby Link Japan
www.hlj.com

Raupen Model
www.raupen-modell.com

AFV Club
Hobby Fan Trading Co., Ltd.
6F., No.183, Sec. 1, Datong Rd., Xizhi City,
Taipei County 221, Taiwan
www.hobbyfan.com.tw

Archer Fine Transfers
PO Box 1277,
Youngsville, NC 27596,
USA
www.archertransfers.com

S & S Models
22 Briar Close
Burnham-on-Sea,
Somerset, TA8 1HU
United Kingdom
www.sandsmodels.com

Tetra Modelworks
18, Dorim-ro 126-gil, Yeongdeungpo-gu,
Seoul, Republic of Korea 150-834
www.tetramodel.co.kr

Hobby Master Ltd
Rm 30, 5/F, Blk A, Cambridge Plaza,188 Sun
Wan Rd, Sheung Shui, N.T., Hong Kong
www.hobbymaster.com.hk

As with the previous books in this series I have endeavoured to give the general reader an understanding of what seems to be a much neglected, yet very important, aspect of the British army's campaign in northern Europe during the last year of the Second World War. In compiling the unit histories I relied heavily on the research of Philip Reinders and also the works of Georges Bernage, Yves Buffetaut, Ronald McNair and Richard C. Anderson. I also used my own research from *British Armour in North-West Europe, Vol.1 Normandy to Arnhem* which was first released in 2008. Much of the information in the technical section was based on the works of Wojciech Gawrych, Steven Zaloga and Bryan Perret. As the M10 was based on the M4A2 Sherman I also consulted R.P. Hunnicutt's *Sherman, A History of the American Medium Tank*, still regarded as the foremost authority on this vehicle. A very helpful online resource was the Sherman Minutia web site, an encyclopaedic, and ever evolving, examination of the Sherman tank compiled by a number of well-known M4 experts including Joe DeMarco and my old friend Leife Hulbert. All the illustrations were based on photographs of actual tanks and I should probably thank Al Bowie here who I consulted on the camouflage possibilities and also some of the markings. Where I have been forced to speculate in the creation of the vehicle profiles I have tried to make this clear. I would like to thank Ramon Segarra and Masanori Sato, two of the talented modellers who graciously allowed me to publish the images of their work, and in particular Luciano Rodriguez who went above and beyond with his RCA Achilles and Chris Camfield who provided the original plan drawings for the turret roof modification. I would also like to thank Rupert Harding and Stephen Chumbley, my editors at Pen & Sword for their advice, assistance and above all patience. Of the product manufacturers I must make special mention of Roberto Reale of Royal Model and Jan Zdiarsky from Eduard Model Accessories. I would also like to mention Ian Carter at the Imperial War Museum's photographic archive and Karl Berne, Valeri Polokov and J.Howard Parker for their invaluable assistance with some of the photographs and period insignia.

ALSO AVAILABLE IN THE TANKCRAFT SERIES

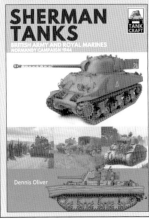

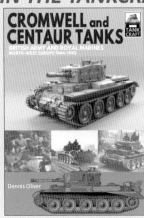

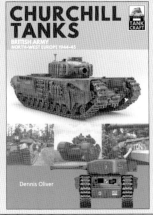

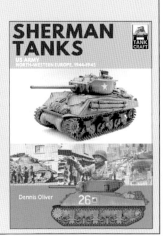